## ALSO BY SUSAN SONTAG

### FICTION

*The Benefactor* · *Death Kit* · *I, etcetera*
*The Way We Live Now* · *The Volcano Lover* · *In America*

### ESSAYS

*Against Interpretation* · *Styles of Radical Will*
*On Photography* · *Illness As Metaphor* · *Under the Sign of Saturn*
*AIDS and Its Metaphors* · *Where the Stress Falls*
*Regarding the Pain of Others* · *At the Same Time*

### FILM SCRIPTS

*Duet for Cannibals* · *Brother Carl*

### PLAY

*Alice in Bed*

*A Susan Sontag Reader*

# REBORN

# REBORN

•

*Journals and Notebooks*

1947–1963

# Susan Sontag

EDITED BY DAVID RIEFF

*Farrar Straus Giroux*

*New York*

*Farrar, Straus and Giroux*
*18 West 18th Street, New York 10011*

*Library of Congress Cataloging-in-Publicaion Data*
Sontag, Susan, 1933–2004.
    *Reborn : journals and notebooks, 1947–1963 / by Susan Sontag;*
*edited by David Rieff.— 1st ed.*
        *p.   cm.*
    *ISBN-13: 978-0-374-10074-2 (alk. paper)*
    *ISBN-10: 0-374-10074-8 (alk. paper)*
    *1. Sontag, Susan, 1933–2004—Diaries.   2. Sontag, Susan,*
*1933–2004—Notebooks, sketchbooks, etc.   3. Authors, American—*
*20th century—Diaries.   4. Women and literature—United States—*
*History—20th century.   I. Rieff, David.   II. Title.*

*PS3569.O6547Z477 2008*
*818'.5409—dc22*

                                                    *2008034247*

*Designed by Dorothy Schmiderer Baker*

*www.fsgbooks.com*

*1  3  5  7  9  10  8  6  4  2*

# Contents

# Preface

I have always thought that one of the stupidest things the living say about the dead is the phrase "so-and-so would have wanted it this way." At best, it is guesswork; most often it is hubris, no matter how well intended. You simply cannot know. So whatever else there is to be said about the publication of *Reborn*, this first of what will eventually be a three-volume selection of Susan Sontag's journals, it is not the book she would have produced—and that assumes she would have decided to publish these diaries in the first place. Instead, both the decision to publish and the selection have been mine alone. Even when there is no question of censorship, the literary dangers and moral hazards of such an enterprise are self-evident. *Caveat lector.*

It is not a decision I ever wanted to make. But my mother died without leaving any instructions as to what to do with either her papers or her uncollected or unfinished writing. This might seem out of character for someone who took such care of her work, who labored furiously on translations even in languages she knew only passably, and had informed and decisive opinions about publishers and magazines the world over. But despite the lethality of myelodysplastic syndrome, the blood cancer that killed her on December 28, 2004, she continued to believe until only a few weeks before her death that she was going to survive. So instead of speaking about how she wanted others to look after her work once she was no longer around to look after it herself—as someone who was more resigned to death probably would have done—she spoke emphatically of returning to work, and of all that she would write once she got out of the hospital.

As far as I am concerned, she had an absolute right to die as she wished. She owed posterity, let alone me, nothing as she fought to live. But obviously there are unintended consequences of her decision—the most important here being that it has devolved to me to decide how to publish the writings she left behind. In the case of her essays, which appeared in *At the Same Time* two years after her death, the choices were relatively straightforward. Despite the fact that my mother certainly would have substantially revised the essays for republication, they had already been either published during her lifetime or delivered as lectures. Her intentions were clear.

These diaries are a completely different matter. They were written solely for herself, and she produced them steadily from early adolescence to the last few years of her life, when her delight in the computer and in e-mail seems to have curbed her interest in diary-keeping. She had never permitted a line from them to be published, nor, unlike some diarists, did she read from them to friends, although those close to her knew of their existence and of her habit after filling a notebook of placing it alongside its predecessors in the walk-in closet in her bedroom, near other treasured but somehow essentially private possessions, such as family photographs and mementos of her childhood.

By the time she fell ill for the last time, in the spring of 2004, there were close to a hundred such notebooks. And others turned up as her last assistant, Anne Jump, and her closest friend, Paolo Dilonardo, and I were sorting through her effects in the year after her death. I had only the vaguest idea of what was in them. The sole conversation I ever had with my mother about them was when she first fell ill and had not yet rekindled her own belief that she would survive her blood cancer as she had the two previous cancers she had suffered from in her lifetime. And it consisted of a single, whispered sentence: "You know where the diaries are." She said nothing about what she wanted me to do with them.

I can't say for sure, but I tend to believe that, left to my own devices, I would have waited a long time before publishing them, or perhaps never published them at all. There have even been times when I've thought that I would burn them. But that was pure fantasy. The reality, in any case, is that the physical diaries do not belong to me. While she was still well, my mother had sold her papers to the University of California at Los Angeles library, and the agreement was that they would go there upon her death, along with her papers and her books, as they have. And since the contract my mother concluded did not restrict access in any important sense, I soon came to feel that the decision had been made for me. Either I would organize them and present them or someone else would. It seemed better to go forward.

My misgivings remain. To say that these diaries are self-revelatory is a drastic understatement. I have chosen to include a lot of my mother's very severe judgments. She was a great "judger." But to expose that quality in her—and these diaries are replete with exposures—is inevitably to invite the reader to judge *her*. One of the principal dilemmas in all this has been that, at least in her later life, my mother was not in any way a self-revealing person. In particular, she avoided to the extent she could, without denying it, any discussion of her own homosexuality or any acknowledgment of her own ambition. So my decision certainly violates her privacy. There is no other way of describing it fairly.

In contrast, these diaries are anchored in her adolescent discovery of her own sexual nature, of early experiments as a sixteen-year-old freshman at the University of California at Berkeley, and of the two great relationships that she had as a young adult—first with a woman identified here as H, whom she first encountered in that year at Cal, and would later live with in Paris in 1957; and then with the playwright Maria Irene Fornes, whom my mother met that same year in Paris (Fornes and H had been lovers previously), in New York between 1959 and 1963, after my mother returned to the United States, divorced my father, and moved to Manhattan.

Once having decided to publish her journals, I had no question of excluding material, be it on the basis of it putting my mother in a certain light or of its sexual frankness or of its unkindness to some who figure in them, although I have chosen to omit the real names of some private individuals. To the contrary, my principle of selection was partly informed by my sense that it was the rawness and the unvarnished portrait this material presents of Susan Sontag as a young person, who self-consciously and determinedly went about creating the self she wanted to be, that was most compelling about the journals. It is for this reason that I have chosen to title this volume *Reborn*, drawing from a phrase that appears on the front of one of the early journals; it seems to sum up what my mother was about from childhood onward.

No American writer of her generation was more associated with European tastes than was my mother. Impossible to imagine her saying that she had "all Tucson" or "all Sherman Oaks, California, to tell," as John Updike has said of his beginnings as a writer that he had all of his hometown of "Shillington [Pennsylvania] to tell." And even more impossible to imagine was my mother returning to her childhood or to her social and ethnic context for inspiration, as many Jewish-American writers of her generation would do. Her story—again, the appositeness of *Reborn* as a title seems to me reinforced—is precisely the opposite. In many ways, it is the same as Lucien de Rubempré's—the ambitious young person from the deep provinces who wants to become a person of significance in the capital.

Of course, my mother was no Rubempré in any other meaning of character, temperament, or project. She did not want to secure favors. To the contrary, she believed in her star. From her early adolescence, she had the sense of having special gifts, and of having something to contribute. The fierce and unremitting desire to constantly deepen and expand her education—a project that occupies so much space in the diaries and that I have tried to include in the same proportions in this selection—was in a way the materialization of this sense of herself. She wanted to be worthy of the writers, painters, and musicians she revered. It was in this sense that Isaac Babel's *mot d'ordre*, "You must know everything," could have been Susan Sontag's as well.

This is the very opposite of the way we think today. A belief in oneself is a constant in the consciousness of those who succeed in the world, but the form of that self-confidence is culturally determined and varies greatly from period to period. My mother's was, I think, a nineteenth-century consciousness, and the self-absorption of these journals has something of the tone of those great, selfish "accomplishers"—Carlyle comes to my mind. And this is far removed from the register in which ambition expresses itself in the early twenty-first century. A reader looking for irony will find none. My mother was profoundly aware of this. In her essay on Elias Canetti, which, along with her piece on Walter Benjamin, I always thought to be as close to a sally into autobiography as she would ever make, she quoted approvingly Canetti's musing, "I try to imagine someone saying to Shakespeare, 'Relax!' "

So again, *caveat lector.* This is a journal where art is seen as a matter of life and death, where irony is assumed to be a vice, not a virtue, and where seriousness is the greatest good. These traits my mother exhibited early. And she never lacked for people who tried to get her to relax. She used to recall that her benevolent and conventional war-hero stepfather had pleaded with her not to read so much lest she never find a husband. The more self-assuredly cultivated version of this was the remark of the philosopher Stuart Hampshire, her tutor at Oxford, whom she told me once had exclaimed in frustration during a tutorial, "Oh, you Americans! You're so serious . . . just like the Germans." He did not mean it as a compliment; but my mother wore it as a badge of honor.

All of this might make a reader think that my mother was a "natural European," in Isaiah Berlin's sense of there being Europeans who were "natural" Americans and Americans who were "natural" Europeans. But I do not think this is quite right in my mother's case. It is true that for her American literature was a suburb of the great literatures of Europe—above all German literature—and yet probably her deepest assumption was that she could remake herself, that we can all remake ourselves, and that backgrounds could be jettisoned or transcended virtually at will, or, rather, if one had the will. And what is this if not the personification of Fitzgerald's observation that "there are no second acts in American lives"? As I say, on her deathbed that she never fully believed would be her deathbed, she was planning the next first act that she would live after the treatment had bought her some more time.

In this, my mother was remarkably consistent. One of the most striking things to me reading her journals was the impression that, from youth to old age, my mother was fighting the same battles, both with the world and with herself. Her feeling of mastery of the arts, her breathtaking confidence in the rightness of her own judgments, her extraordinary avidity—the sense that she needed to hear every piece of music, see every artwork, be conversant with all the great works of literature—are there from the start, when she is listing books she wants to read and then ticking them off as she reads them. But so is her sense of failure, of unsuitability for love and even for eros. She was as uncomfortable with her body as she was serene about her mind.

That makes me sadder than I can possibly convey. When my mother was very young, she took a trip to Greece. There, she saw a performance of *Medea* in an amphitheater in southern Peloponnesus. The experience moved her profoundly because as Medea is about to kill her children, a number of people in the audience started yelling, "No, don't do it, Medea!" "These people had no sense of seeing a work of art," she told me many times. "It was all real."

These diaries are real, too. And reading them, I have very much the anxiety that I am responding as those Greek spectators in the mid-1950s did. I want to shout, "Don't do it" or else "Don't be so hard on yourself" or "Don't think so well of yourself" or "Watch out for her, she doesn't love you." But of course I am too late: the play has already been performed and its protagonist is gone, as are most though not all of the other characters as well.

What remains is pain and ambition. These journals oscillate between them. Would my mother have wanted them exposed? Again, there are practical reasons behind my decision not only to allow their publication but to edit them myself, even if there are things contained in them that are a source of pain to me, and much that I would have preferred not to know and not to have others know.

What I do know is that as a reader and a writer my mother loved diaries and letters—the more intimate the better. So perhaps Susan Sontag the writer would have approved of what I've done. I hope so, at any rate.

DAVID RIEFF

# REBORN

# 1947

11/23/47

I believe:

(a) That there is no personal god or life after death

(b) That the most desirable thing in the world is freedom to be true to oneself, i.e., Honesty

(c) That the only difference between human beings is intelligence

(d) That the only criterion of an action is its ultimate effect on making the individual happy or unhappy

(e) That it is wrong to deprive any man of life
 [*Entries "f" and "g" are missing.*]

(h) I believe, furthermore, that an ideal state (besides "g") should be a strong centralized one with government control of public utilities, banks, mines, + transportation and subsidy of the arts, a comfortable minimum wage, support of disabled and age[d]. State care of pregnant women with no distinction such as legitimate + illegitimate children.

# 1948

4/13/48

Ideas disturb the levelness of life

7/29/48

. . . And what is it to be young in years and suddenly wakened to the anguish, the urgency of life?

It is to be reached one day by the reverberations of those who do not follow, to stumble out of the jungle and fall into an abyss:

It is then to be blind to the faults of the rebellious, to yearn painfully, wholly, after all opposites of childhood's existence. It is impetuousness, wild enthusiasm, immediately submerged in a flood of self-deprecation. It is the cruel awareness of one's own presumption . . .

It is humiliation with every slip-of-the-tongue, sleepless nights spent rehearsing tomorrow's conversation, and torturing oneself for yesterday's . . . a bowed head held between one's hands . . . it is "my god, my god" . . . (in lower case, of course, because there is no god).

It is withdrawal of feeling toward one's family and all childhood idols . . . It is lying . . . and resentment, and then hate . . .

It is the emergence of cynicism, a probing of every thought and word and action. ("Ah, to be perfectly, utterly sincere!") It is a bitter and relentless questioning of motives . . .

It is to discover that the catalyst, the [*Entry trails off at this point.*]

8/19/48

What seemed once to be a crushing weight has sharply shifted position, in a surprising tactic, swung beneath my fleeing feet, become a sucking force that drags and tires me. How I long to surrender! How easy it would be to convince myself of the plausibility of my parents' life! If I saw only them and their friends for a year, would resign myself— surrender? Does my "intelligence" need frequent rejuvenation at the springs of *other's* dissatisfaction and die without it? If I can hold myself to these vows! For I can feel myself slipping, wavering—at certain times, even accepting the idea of staying home for college.

All I can think of is Mother, how pretty she is, what smooth skin she has, how she loves me. How she shook when she cried the other night—she didn't want Dad, in the other room, to hear her, and the noise of each choked wave of tears was like a giant hiccup—what cowards people are to involve themselves, rather, to passively let themselves be involved, by convention, in sterile relationships—what rotten, dreary, miserable lives they lead—

How can I hurt her more, beaten as she is, *never* resisting?

How can I help me, make me cruel?

9/1/48

What does the expression "in his cups" mean?

Stone-slung mountain.

Read the [Stephen] Spender translation of [Rilke's] *The Duino Elegies* as soon as possible.

Immersing myself in Gide again—what clarity and precision! Truly it is the man himself who is incomparable—all his fiction seems insignificant, while [Mann's] *The Magic Mountain* is a book for all of one's life.

I know that! *The Magic Mountain* is the finest novel I've ever read. The sweetness of renewed and undiminishing acquaintance with this work, the peaceful and meditative pleasure I feel are unparalleled. Yet for sheer emotional impact, for a sense of *physical* pleasure, an awareness of quick breath and quickly wasted lives—hurrying, hurrying—for the knowledge of life—no, not that—for a knowledge of aliveness—I would choose [Romain Rolland's] *Jean-Christophe*—But it should only be read once.

•

... "When I am dead, I hope it may be said:
'His sins were scarlet, but his books were read.' "

—Hilaire Belloc

•

Immersed myself in Gide all afternoon and listened to the [conductor Fritz] Busch (Glyndebourne festival) recording of [Mozart's] *Don Giovanni.* Several arias (such soul-stretching sweetness!) I played over and over again ("Mi tradi quell' alma ingrata" and "Fuggi, crudele, fuggi"). If I could always hear them, how resolute and serene I would be!

Wasted the evening with Nat [*Nathan Sontag, SS's step-father*]. He gave me a driving lesson and then I accompanied him and pretended to enjoy a Technicolor blood-and-thunder movie.

After writing this last sentence, I read it again and consider[ed] erasing it. I should let it stand, though.—It is useless for me to record only the satisfying parts of my existence—(There are too few of them anyway!) Let me note all the sickening waste of today, that I shall not be easy with myself and compromise my tomorrows.

9/2/48

A tearful discussion with Mildred [*Mildred Sontag, née Jacobson, SS's mother*] (damn it!). She said, "You should be very happy I married Nat. You would never be going to

Chicago, rest assured of that! I can't tell you how unhappy I am about it, but I feel that I have to make up to you for this."

Maybe I should be glad!!!

9/10/48

*[Written and dated on the inside cover of SS's copy of the second volume of Andre Gide's* Journals*]*

I finished reading this at 2:30 a.m. of the same day I acquired it—

I should have read it much more slowly and I must re-read it many times—Gide and I have attained such perfect intellectual communion that I experience the appropriate labor pains for every thought he gives birth to! Thus I do not think: "How marvelously lucid this is!"—but: "Stop! I cannot think this fast! Or rather I cannot grow this fast!"

For, I am not only reading this book, but creating it myself, and this unique and enormous experience has purged my mind of much of the confusion and sterility that has clogged it all these horrible months—

12/19/48

There are so many books and plays and stories I have to read—Here are just a few:

    *The Counterfeiters*—Gide
    *The Immoralist*— "

*Lafcadio's Adventures*— "
*Corydon*—Gide

*Tar*—Sherwood Anderson
*The Island Within*—Ludwig Lewisohn
*Sanctuary*—William Faulkner
*Esther Waters*—George Moore
*Diary of a Writer*—Dostoyevsky
*Against the Grain*—Huysmans
*The Disciple*—Paul Bourget
*Sanin*—Mikhail Artsybashev
*Johnny Got His Gun*—Dalton Trumbo
*The Forsyte Saga*—Galsworthy
*The Egoist*—George Meredith
*Diana of the Crossways*— "
*The Ordeal of Richard Feverel*— "

poems of Dante, Ariosto, Tasso, Tibullus, Heine, Pushkin, Rimbaud, Verlaine, Apollinaire

plays of Synge, O'Neill, Calderón, Shaw, Hellman . . .
[*This list goes on for another five pages, and more than a hundred titles are mentioned.*]

•

. . . Poetry must be: exact, intense, concrete, significant, rhythmical, formal, complex

. . . Art, then, is thus always striving to be independent of the mere intelligence . . .

. . . Language is not only an instrument but an end in itself . . .

. . . Through the immense and narrowly channeled clarity of his mind, Gerard Hopkins word-wrought a world of wracked and exultant imagery.

Wielding his pitiless lucidity, shielding himself from fleshiness by the rigid spiritualization of his life and art, he yet created work, within its limited scope, of unsurpassed freshness. Upon the anguished issue of his soul . . .

12/25/48

I'm completely engrossed, at this moment, in one of the most beautiful musical works I've ever heard—the Vivaldi B Minor p[iano]f[orte] concerto on Cetra-Soria with Mario Salerno—

Music is at once the most wonderful, the most alive of all the arts—it is the most abstract, the most perfect, the most pure—and the most sensual. I listen with my body and it is my body that aches in response to the passion and pathos embodied in this music. It is the physical "I" that feels an unbearable pain—and then a dull fretfulness—when the whole world of melody suddenly glistens and comes cascading down in the second part of the first movement—it is flesh and bone that dies a little each time I am sucked into the yearning of the second movement—

I am almost on the verge of madness. Sometimes—I think—(how deliberately I pen these words)—there are fleeting (oh so quickly flown) moments when I know as surely as today is Christmas that I am tottering over an illimitable precipice—

What, I ask, drives me to disorder? How can I diagnose myself? All I feel, most immediately, is the most anguished need for *physical love* and mental companionship—I am very young, and perhaps the disturbing aspect of my sexual ambitions will be outgrown—*frankly, I don't care.* [*In the margin, and dated May 31, 1949, SS adds the words: "Nor should you."*] My need is so overwhelming and time, in my obsession, so short—

I shall, in all probability, look back on this with a great deal of amusement. Just as I was once terrifiedly and neurotically religious and thought I should one day become a Catholic, so now I feel that I have lesbian tendencies (how reluctantly I write this)—

I must not think of the solar system—of innumerable galaxies spanned by countless light years—of infinities of space—I must not look up at the sky for longer than a moment—I must not think of death, of forever—I must not do all those things so that I will not know these horrible moments when my mind seems a tangible thing—more than my mind—my whole spirit—all that animates me and is the original and responsive desire that constitutes my "self"—all this takes on a definite shape and size—far too large to be contained by the structure I call my body—All this pulls and pushes—years and strains (I feel it now) until I must clench my fists—I rise—who can keep still—every muscle is on a rack—striving to build itself into an immensity—I want to scream—my stomach feels compressed—my legs, feet, toes stretching until they hurt.

I come closer and closer to bursting this poor shell—I know it now—contemplation of infinity—the straining of my mind drives me to dilute the horror by the opposite of abstraction's simple sensuality. *And knowing that I do not possess the outlet, some demon nevertheless torments me—brims me with pain and fury—with fear and trembling (wrenched, racked I am—most wretched—) my mind mastered by spasms of uncontrollable desire—*

12/31/48

I read again these notebooks. How dreary and monotonous they are! Can I never escape this interminable mourning for myself? My whole being seems tense—expectant . . .

# 1949

1/25/49

I am going to Cal for this semester if I can get into a dorm.

2/11/49

*[SS is writing just before she leaves her home in Los Angeles about her decision to attend Berkeley.]*

. . . Emotionally, I wanted to stay. Intellectually, I wanted to leave. As always, I seemed to enjoy punishing myself.

2/19/49

*[SS has arrived at "Cal," the University of California, Berkeley; she is barely sixteen.]*

Well, I'm here.

It's no different at all; it seems it never was a matter of finding more felicitous surroundings, but of finding myself—
finding self-esteem and personal integrity.

I'm no happier now than I was at home—. . .

. . . I want to write—*I want to live in an intellectual atmosphere*—I want to live in a cultural center where I can hear a
great deal of music—all this and much more, but . . . the
important thing is that there seems to be no profession better
suited to my needs than university teaching . . . [*Across the
remark about teaching, SS later scrawled: "Jesus!"*]

3/1/49

I bought *Point Counter Point* today and read steadily for six
hours to finish it. [Aldous] Huxley's prose is so deliciously
assured—his observations so gloriously acute, if one glories
in the deft exposing of our civilization's emptiness—I found
the book very exciting, though—a tribute to my embryonic
critical abilities. I revel even in the inevitable depression
which follows the reading of the book, simply because I have
been aroused to a barren agitation in such a skillful manner!

Virtuosity impresses me more than anything else at this
moment of my life—Technique, organization, verbal luxuri-
ance appeal to me most strongly. The cruelly realistic comment (Huxley, Rochefoucauld)—the mocking caricature, or
the lengthy, sensuous philosophic exposition of Thomas
Mann in *Der Zauberberg* and [*Der*] *Tod in Venedig* [*The
Magic Mountain* and *Death in Venice*] . . . Very narrow
of me—

•

"The problem for me is to transform a detached
intellectual scepticism into a way of harmonious
all-round living."

*P[oin]t Counter P[oin]t*

•

4/2/49

I am in love with being in love!—Whatever I can think of
Irene [*Lyons, lover of H., becomes SS's lover and plays an
important role in the journals from 1957 to 1963*] when I do
not see her—Whatever intellectual restraint I can imagine
myself possessed of—vanishes with the pain + frustration I
feel in her presence. It is not an easy thing to be rejected so
utterly—

4/6/49

I have not been able to bring myself to write of this until I
had achieved some temporal + psychic distance—

What I know is very ugly—and so unbearable because it
cannot be communicated—I tried! I wanted to respond! I
wanted so much to feel a physical attraction for him and
prove, at least, that I am bisexual—[*In the margin, dated
May 31, SS has added: "What a stupid thought!—'at least
bisexual.'"*]

. . . Nothing but humiliation and degradation at the thought
of physical relations with a man—The first time I kissed

him—a very long kiss—I thought quite distinctly: "Is this all?—it's so silly"—I tried! I did try—but I know now it can never be—I want to hide—Oh, and I've messed up Peter's life so—

His name is James Rowland Lucas—Jim—it was Friday evening, March 11th—the night I had planned to attend a Mozart concert in San Francisco.

•

What am I to do? [*In another, this time undated, later "comment," SS has written: "Enjoy yourself, of course."*]

[*Certainly written in April 1949, but undated in the notebook*]

Going home for a weekend was an amazing experience. I felt in myself a further emotional emancipation from what I—intellectually—find flawed—I think I am finally free of my dependence on / affection for Mother—She aroused nothing in me, not even pity—just boredom—The house never seemed as small, nor everyone so innately dull and trivial, and my own vitality was oppressive—Here, at least [*e.g., at Berkeley*], in undisguised aloneness, I have figured some pleasures and compensations—in music and books and reading poetry aloud. I need pretend to no one; I dispose of my time as I wish—At home there are all the pretenses and rituals of amicability—the terrifying waste of time—I must deal with the time of this summer carefully, for there is much to accomplish—

If I am not accepted at Chicago [*after one term at the University of California, Berkeley, SS had applied to transfer to the*

*College of the University of Chicago*], and, consequently plan to return to Cal in the winter, I shall stay up here for the first summer session. If not, then I shall audit these courses in the UCLA 8-week session.

2:00–5:00 every day I shall set aside for writing and study outside in the sun, and whatever time in the evenings I can manage—I shall be quiet, courteous, and disinvolved!

4/8/49

This afternoon, I heard a lecture on "The Function of Art and the Artist" by Anaïs Nin: she is very startling—pixie-like, other-worldly—small, finely-built, dark hair, and much make-up which made her look very pale—large, questioning eyes—a marked accent which I could not label—her speech is over-precise—she shines and polishes each syllable with the very tip of her tongue and teeth—one feels that if one were to touch her, she would crumble into silver dust. [*In the margin, SS later writes: "H was there."*]

Her theory of art was preciously intangible (discovery-of-the-unconscious, automatic-writing, revolt-against-our-mechanistic-civilization)—She was analyzed by Otto Rank.

4/14/49

I read [Djuna Barnes's] *Nightwood* yesterday—What a great prose she writes—That is the way I want to write—rich and rhythmic—heavy, sonorous prose that befits those mythic ambiguities that are both source and structure to an aesthetic experience symbolized by language—

4/16/49

I read the major part of [Dostoyevsky's] *The Brothers Kara-mazov* and suddenly feel frantically impure. I wrote three letters to Peter and Audrey completely severing those relationships and to Mother, semi-declaring my revulsion for the past—

●

Oh, it was Irene, too—

She's right and admirable, to be honest—

●

And to think I had talked myself into affection for Peter, because I was so lonely and I couldn't imagine finding anyone better than he! And all that mess with Audrey—Hell, if Irene can be honest and reject me—I can (for the first time) be sincere myself—

*[On the inside cover page of the notebook dated 5/7/49– 5/31/49, SS writes in capital letters: "I AM REBORN IN THE TIME RETOLD IN THIS NOTEBOOK."]*

5/17/49

Finished [Hermann Hesse's] *Demian* today and was, on the whole, greatly disappointed. The book has some very fine passages, and the first few chapters describing Sinclair's early adolescence are quite good . . . But the straight-faced supernaturalism of the latter part of the book is a shock by the realistic standards implicit in the earlier part of the book. It's not the Romantic tone I object to (for I loved [Goethe's *Sorrows of Young*] *Werther*, for instance) but Hesse's (I can express it no other way) childishness of conception . . .

I am beginning Rudolf Steiner's *The Theory of Knowledge Implicit in Goethe's World-Conception*. I seem to be following the thought without effort so I'm doubly suspicious of myself and read very slowly . . .

Also within the last few weeks (have I already noted this?) I have read the Bayard Taylor [translation of] Part I of [Goethe's] *Faust*, the [Christopher] Marlowe [*Doctor*] *Faustus*, and the Mann novel—

I was very moved by the Goethe, although I think I'm far from understanding it—the Marlowe is just about *mine* though—for I've put a good deal of time into it, re-reading it several times, and declaiming many of the passages aloud again and again. Faustus' final soliloquy I have read aloud a dozen times in the past week. It is incomparable . . .

Somewhere, in an earlier notebook, I confessed a disappointment with the Mann [*Doctor*] *Faustus* . . . This was a uniquely undisguised evidence of the quality of my critical sensibility! The work is a great and satisfying one, which I'll have to read many times before I can possess it . . .

I'm re-reading pieces of things that have always been important to me, and am amazed at my evaluations. A good deal of [Gerard Manley] Hopkins yesterday, and I wasn't as enthused as I've always been—I particularly felt the letdown in the "Leaden Echo" [and] "Golden Echo" poems—

It is so good to read *aloud*—I'm also re-reading (with undiminished pleasure) the Dante, and [T. S.] Eliot (of course) . . .

This summer I want to concentrate on Aristotle, Yeats, Hardy, and Henry James . . .

5/18/49

Will I never learn from my own stupidity! I heard today a lecture-recital on Browning's dramatic monologues . . . How ignorant of and snobbish about Browning I've always been!—Another author to work with this summer . . .

5/23/49

*[This entry, which runs almost thirty pages, was meant to recapitulate a whole period of SS's life at Berkeley, ending with her meeting H. and, through her, beginning to take part in gay life in San Francisco.]*

This weekend has been a beautifully patterned summation, and, I think, partial resolution of my greatest unhappiness: the agonized dichotomy between the body and the mind that has had me on the rack for the past two years: It is, perhaps, the most important space of time—(important to whatever I will be as a whole person)—I've known.

On Friday evening I went with Al [*SS notes: Allan Cox*] to hear a paper by George Boas, a visiting professor of philosophy from Johns Hopkins, entitled "Meaning in the Arts." It was an entertainingly glib paper, exposing the faults of the major critical schools since and including Aristotle, but con-

structing nothing very tangible of his own—just this witty
and sterile perception of manifold error. Several interesting
things: spoke of the evolution of art in terms of a fluctuation
between *ritual* and *improvisation*—a nice-sounding restate-
ment of the overworked Classic vs. Romantic antithesis . . .
One shot of his was directed at the Aristotelean critics who
refuse to comprehend the fact that Aristotle did not know
anything about Shakespeare, and therefore can't understand
how *Hamlet* manages to be a tragedy (true tragedy = Aristotle's delimitations) but know emotionally it is, or else
pretend that, in some occult way, it really is a tragedy in
Aristotle's terms . . .

Al himself, and my relationship to him, really personify all
my longing to retreat to the intellect, all my fears and inhi-
bitions concerning life. He is twenty-two, ex–merchant
marine—didn't get into the army because of color blind-
ness—extremely handsome in the classic sense—tall, curly
brown hair, perfect features except for very attractively
flared nostrils—beautiful hands . . . Comes from a small
town (Santa Ana) where he lived all his life until he came to
Berkeley at 18 to go to Cal, his college career being interrupted by three years at sea. Academically, he's a junior,
and a chemistry major, although his major interests are
math and literature. He wants to write, but doesn't dare to
because he's afraid it would be very bad—and it probably
would. He is very good in math, and, if he could muster
the self-confidence would attempt to insinuate himself
into Philosophy through this study. His background is a
Lutheran-German one—he has a real medieval mind: his
overwhelming humility and sense of sin, his love of knowledge and *abstraction*, his total subordination of the body to
what he considers important: the mind. On a recent date he
confessed to me that he hadn't eaten all day just to discipline

himself. He has, I think, a very *capable* mind—one of the finest intellects I've yet come in contact with—Although it's absurd to imagine him a virgin, yet I'm sure he is normally wholly continent, and feels tremendously guilty about his rare lapses into sin . . .

I first met him near the beginning of the semester, when I noticed him at a record concert (*Don Giovanni* complete), and realized he was a hasher [*sic*] here at the dorms. We talked casually, met again at several other concerts, and, then, after weeks of tight-lipped, languishing glances, he was brave enough to ask me to a concert with him (the *Magnificat* [Bach] at the local Congregational church).—Since then, what few cultural things I've attended have been with him, and just to be with another person, however bloodless the relationship might be, distracted me from the humiliating denouement of my relationship with Irene. I was never physically attracted to Al, and I was comfortable with him for two reasons: I genuinely respected his intelligence and wanted to learn from him and discuss music and literature and philosophy with him; also I knew it would take him weeks to make any physical overtures, and it would, at such a time in the future, be simple to disinvolve myself. As yet, we haven't even held hands! I *did* feel comfortable with him—though not affirmative and alive. The *horrible* thing was that, on this Friday night, I almost convinced myself that the intellectual satisfaction I felt with him—which was simply an absence of pain—was good, and the best kind of satisfaction there was—After Boas we sat over coffee for an hour, and then, walking, talked for two or three more hours.

We discussed everything from Bach cantatas to Mann's *Faustus* to pragmatism to hyperbolic functions to the Cal Labor School to Einstein's theory of curved space. It was the math-philosophy that was so fascinating. Right then I genuinely shared his deep humility and relaxed grasp on life—he is not afraid to die, simply because he knows how unimportant his life, human life is—We both talked brilliantly, and everything seemed very clear to me because, at that moment, I had rejected more than I ever had: the totality of wandering and laziness and sun and sex and food and sleep and music . . . I felt very confident that my decision to teach was right, that nothing really mattered except acceptable and mentally-digested experiences . . . Simply, that nothing really mattered too much. I was, at that moment, very little afraid to die . . . We said that one should always expect the worst in life—life being one long sordidness and mediocrity—that one should not protest, but, although assuming the necessary social responsibilities, withdraw, not involve oneself, and, in the anticipation of the worst, perhaps be granted a few moments of happiness: not accepting life "conditionally" was what I said . . . Take what you can— none of it really matters . . . I believed it! . . . I felt good about it . . . Irene seemed distant, too . . . I felt truly at peace as I left him at the dorm entrance (with our studied camaraderie) and walked upstairs to sleep . . .

I could win out yet against life—against my own passionateness—I would resign it all—"resign them, sign them, seal them, deliver up to God . . ." [*SS is partly quoting, partly paraphrasing a line from Gerard Manley Hopkins's dialogue poem "The Leaden Echo and the Golden Echo."*]

Saturday morning, as usual, I awakened at 9:30 to make my "Age of [Samuel] Johnson" audit at 10:00. (When I filled up my hours with audits at the beginning of the term, I had noticed this class, which meets TuThs 10, but, of course, I have French five hours a week at 10:00—Toward the middle

of the term—late March—I got to talking with a girl
named H who worked at the Campus Textbook Exchange—
I talked very easily with her—(I usually can, the first time I
meet a stranger)—she told me how good the Johnson class
was, so I started coming just on Saturdays, and got a great
deal from it—oh, the fanatic concentration on the *awesome*
trivia of the 18th century!—The lecturer, Mr. Bronson, is a
terribly civilized man, T. S. Eliotish–looking, English accent,
dry humor, low voice, quiet way of moving . . . (He thinks it's
simply catastrophic that most people think badly of Boswell,
etc. . . .)

. . . H is quite tall—about 5'11"—not pretty, but attractive
just the same—She has a beautiful smile, and is, it was obvious to me, the minute I first talked to her—wonderfully,
uniquely alive . . . After I started coming to the Johnson class,
I used to talk with her after each Saturday, and sometimes at
the bookstore. Before vacation she asked me if I'd like to
come with her to an "ethnic supper" at the room of one of
her friends . . . The guy turned out to be an insufferable, ill-
mannered (the smiling way) homosexual . . . His mother had
sent him some lox and schmaltz and matzohs! The few other
Berkeley bohemians there were very dull, and I acted pretty
inanely myself—my sardonic-intellectual-snob pose; and I
was very conscious of it all the time . . . At that time, H told
me that the best people in San Francisco were at the bars,
and that someday she'd take me with her . . . Last Thursday,
the 19th, I wandered into the bookstore (bought some
French poetry) and she repeated that invitation—I, of
course, accepting—and we made it for this Saturday night . . .
I came down to the Johnson class, then, signed out until
2:30 a.m.—lockout time on Saturdays. After the class was
over, she suggested that I come over with her on Sunday to
Sausalito, where her friend, a girl named A, lived . . .

. . . I was very surprised that she asked me to come with her—she, naturally, herself immediately regretted it, but when I gave her an out, she still reiterated the invitation. I left her there, she to go to work, I to eat lunch . . .

. . . I killed the afternoon at a badly-done student production of three one-acts at Cal Hall, and then came by the bookstore at 5:30. We walked over to her room, and while she changed into levis, I read the first pages of her copy of [Hermann Hesse's] *Steppenwolf* . . . I was wonderfully at ease with her and on the F train over to S[an] F[rancisco] I found myself wanting very much to tell her about Irene. As I did, I realized how diametrically opposed she and her world was to Irene and Al, they of purity and intellect! I told her that, too, and her reaction to the whole business was so different from any of my thoughts . . . I had to laugh, it was so absurd! She said Irene was a bitch—that when she told me how ugly I was I should have said something really obscene so she would have to come down from her holy attitude—that she was narrow and insensitive and not alive . . . In a way—only partially then—I felt H to be right . . . That I was not horrible . . . And I need so to be rid of that consciousness of being sinful . . . We went to a Chinese place for a filling, cheap dinner . . . While we were [finishing], A and her husband, B, came in . . . [then] the four of us went to a bar called Mona's. Most of the people there were lesbian couples . . . the singer was a very tall and beautiful blonde in a strapless evening gown, and even though I wondered about her remarkably powerful voice, H—smilingly—had to *tell* me she was a man . . . There were two other singers—an enormous woman—one of the fattest I've ever seen—she just extended forever in all directions—and a man of medium height—dark Italian face—who, at this point, a little more observant, I know to be a woman . . .

The juke-box was playing and A and B, and, once or twice, B and H, danced. The first time I danced with H I was very tense and stepped all over her feet . . . The second time it was much easier and I began to feel rather good . . .

We had a beer, and then, when we walked out, A and B left us—we were to meet them around 12:30 at a place called the Paper Doll . . . It was now about 11:30 . . . First, though, H wanted to go to a bar down the street called 12 Adler (Henri, the owner, wears a beret) and among the many people whom she knew there was a lewd old man of about 60 named Otto, whom she invited to come with us because, she told me later, he always pays for the drinks. We went down to the Paper Doll then and sat around there until they closed at 2:00 . . . B and A came in about 1:15 . . . There was no show, just some god-awful pianist named Madeleine who insisted on banging out *and* singing everything from "Happy Birthday" on up! She stopped around a quarter of two, and I danced with H again . . . Besides the four of us and Otto there were two other people (independent of each other) who were sitting with us—a young fellow named John Dever, who apparently roomed above the P.D., and a beautiful girl—very dressed— named Roberta—

There were several attractive women who served the drinks—all in men's clothes, as at Mona's—Otto fulfilled his function and bought four rounds for all of us . . . and he was very annoying to me—it seemed I was to be the target this evening, and he kept talking, and I wasn't listening . . . When we left, I found out that B was going to stay in the city all night . . . He left us, forgetting to give A the keys to their Model A, and when A went after him, H and I sat in the car + held hands . . . She was rather drunk, and I, although

I had been downing them as fast as they came, completely sober, but feeling very good and right . . .

The ride to Sausalito is over the Golden Gate Bridge, and while A and H were sitting next to me and necking, I watched the bay and felt warm and alive . . . I had never truly comprehended that it *was* possible to live through your body and not make any of these hideous *dichotomies* after all!

. . . H and I [finally] went in to sleep on a narrow cot in the back of the Tin Angel . . .

Perhaps I was drunk, after all, because it was so beautiful when H began making love to me . . . It had been 4:00 before we had gotten to bed—and we'd talked for a while . . . The first time H kissed me, I was still stiff, but this time it was just because I didn't know how, not that I didn't like it (as with Jim) . . . She made some crack about the enamel of her teeth being gone now—we talked some more, and just when I became fully conscious that I desired her, she knew it, too . . .

Everything that was so tight, that hurt so in the pit of my stomach, was vanquished in the straining against her, the weight of her body on top of mine, the caress of her mouth and her hands . . .

*I knew everything then, nor have I forgotten it now . . .*

. . . And what am I now, as I write this? Nothing less than an entirely different person . . . The experience of this weekend could not have been more perfectly timed—And *I was*

*so close to completely negating myself* of surrendering altogether. My concept of sexuality is so altered—Thank god!—
bisexuality as the expression of fullness of an individual—
and an honest rejection of the—yes—perversion which
limits sexual experience, attempts to de-physicalize it, in
such concepts as the idealization of chastity until the "right
person" comes along—the whole ban on pure physical sensation without love, *on promiscuity* . . .

I know now a little of my capacity . . . I know what I want to
do with my life, all of this being so simple, but so difficult
for me in the past to know. I want to sleep with many people—I want to live and hate to die—I will *not* teach, or get
a master's after I get my B.A. . . . I don't intend to let my
intellect dominate me, and the last thing I want to do is wor-
ship knowledge or people who have knowledge! I don't give a
damn for *anyone's* aggregation of facts, except in that it be
a reflection [of] basic sensitivity which I do demand . . . I
intend to do everything . . . to have one way of evaluating
experience—does it cause me pleasure or pain, and I shall be
very cautious about rejecting the painful—I shall anticipate
pleasure everywhere and find it, too, for it *is* everywhere! I
shall involve myself wholly . . . *everything matters!* The only
thing I resign is the power to resign, to retreat: the acceptance of sameness and the intellect. I am alive . . . I am beautiful . . . what else is there?

5/24/49

I do not think it possible to surrender what I know now . . .
I feared a relapse, but even wedged back into the routine, I
still have the answer of which I was so sure in the wake of
an ecstasy . . . I watch Irene, so obvious in her confusion and

avoidance of me . . . her mouth is so thin . . . It's really sad to realize how incomplete she is, how miserable she'll always be . . . It isn't that I've stopped loving her—it's just that she's been completely diminished, eclipsed by the wonderful widening of my world which I owe to H . . . I have made so few right decisions, and most of those right for the wrong reasons . . . My letter to Irene, for instance, contained much truth though I did not mean the true interpretation of those grand phrases . . .

To love one's body and use it well, that's primary . . . I can do that, I know, for I am freed now . . .

5/25/49

A thought occurred to me today—so obvious, so always obvious! It was absurd to suddenly comprehend it for the first time—I felt rather giddy, a little hysterical:—There is nothing, nothing that stops me from doing *anything* except myself . . . What is to prevent me from just picking up and taking off? Just the *self*-enforced pressures of my environment, but which have always seemed so omnipotent that I never dared to contemplate a violation of them . . . But actually, what stops me? A fear of my family—Mother, especially? A clinging to security and material possessions? Yes, it is both of those, but only those realities that keep me . . . What is college? I can learn nothing, for that which I want to know I can accumulate, and have done so, on my own, and the rest will always be drudgery . . . College is safety, because it is the easy, secure thing to do . . . As for Mother, I honestly don't care—I just don't want to see her—The love of possessions—books and records—those are two oppressions which have been very powerful in me the last few years, yet what,

what bars me from putting my papers, notebooks, and a couple of books in a small box, sending them to a storage company in another city, getting into a couple of shirts and my levis, stuffing another pair of socks and a couple of bucks in my coat pocket, walking out of the house—after leaving an appropriately Byronesque note to the world—and taking a bus—anywhere?—Of course, I'd be caught by the police the first time and sent back to the bosom of my distraught family, but when I walked out the day after I was sent home, and did the same if I were returned again, they would leave me alone—*I can do anything!* Let me make a bargain with myself then—if I am not accepted in Chicago, I will leave in exactly this manner this summer. If I am accepted, then I will go for this next year, and if I am in any way dissatisfied—if in any sense I feel that most of me isn't being used there, then I'll take off—God, living is enormous!

5/26/49

With my new eyes I re-survey the life around me. Most particularly I become frightened to realize how close I came to letting myself slide into the academic life. It would have been effortless . . . just keep on making good grades—(I probably would have stayed in English—I just don't have the math ability for Philosophy)—stayed for a master's and a teaching assistantship, wrote a couple of papers on obscure subjects that nobody cares about, and, at the age of sixty, be ugly and respected and a full professor. Why, I was looking through the English Dept. publications in the library today—long (hundreds of pages) monographs on such subjects as: The Use of "Tu" and "Vous" in Voltaire; The Social Criticism of Fenimore Cooper; A Bibliography of the Writings of Bret Harte in the Magazines + Newspapers of California (1859–1891) . . .

Jesus Christ! What did I almost submit to?!?

5/27/49

Some regression—confusion—today, but that I can recognize [that] it is good at least . . . fear, fear . . . It was Irene, of course: how childish she is, but how inexcusably immature I am! Everything was fine as long as I felt she had completely rejected me . . . Then, last night, just before I left for a philosophy lecture, she walked up to me and said she had decided (!) that she'd like to get to know me some day . . .

5/28/49

*I HAVE BEEN ACCEPTED TO CHICAGO WITH A SCHOLARSHIP OF $765*

•

A opened the Tin Angel last night and H asked me to come. Until I got drunk I thought it all rather depressing—H was high right away, and spent the evening being hysterically amiable to all the women whom she'd slept with during the last year (and now loathed): they all seemed to be there . . . Mary's old girl-friend was, too, looking very sullen . . . B and A got very drunk, naturally, and broke one of the windows . . . I can imagine what they're saying this morning! . . . After a million other people, H got around to necking with me, which was, to put it mildly, lots of fun . . . Then up came some creep (H had been shouting all over the room: "She's only 16—isn't that amazing? And I'm her first lover"), who wanted to "rescue" me . . . H pushed me at him ("Have some heterosexual experience, Sue") and before I knew it we were dancing and necking . . . [*In the margin, SS notes: "Tim Young."*] He gave me a beautiful line which was, I think, somewhat sincere, but when he asked me if I believed in God, I should have spit in his eye . . . But I didn't, damn it, I gave him my telephone number—it was the only way he'd leave me alone—and went back to the front [of the nightclub]. I found myself sitting with three women: one named C, a lawyer, around 34 years old, "distingué" as H kept repeating, born and brought up in California, who had a fake British accent which periodically became noticeable and then was snatched back into her unconscious, and a Crosley car . . . H told me she'd lived with her for two months, until C bought a gun and threatened to shoot them both . . . The other two women were a couple named Florence and Roma . . . H had had an affair with Florence . . . At one point C began to laugh and asked us if we realized what a parody of *Nightwood* this all was . . . It was, of course, and I had, with much amusement, thought of that many times before . . .

[*In an otherwise blank page in the middle of this account, SS writes: "Read* Moll Flanders.*"*]

5/30/49

Corny, juvenile as it may seem, I cannot resist copying some quatrains from the *Rubaiyat* [of Omar Khayyam], because they so perfectly express my present emotional exultation . . .

5/31/49

I re-read, too, the Lucretius that I copied in Notebook #4—
"Life lives on . . . It is the lives, the lives, the lives, that die."

It is good for me to periodically re-read the notebooks that
have preceded this—I note this, written last Christmas day:
And knowing that I do not possess the outlet, some daemon
nevertheless torments me—brims me with pain and fury—
with fear and trembling—(wrenched, wracked I am—most
wretched): my mind mastered by spasms of uncontrollable
desire—

I have come very far since then—learning how to "let go"—
how to possess a moment more fully, more widely—accepting my self, aye, rejoicing in my self—

The really important thing is not to reject anything—When
I think how I wavered about actually coming up to Cal! That
I actually considered not accepting this new experience!
How disastrous (although I would have never known!) that
would have been—

I'll really know what to do in Chicago when I get there—I'll
begin right by going out and grabbing at experience, not
waiting for it to come to me—I can do that now because the
Great Barrier is down—*the feeling of sanctity about my
body*—I have always been full of lust—as I am now—but
I have always been placing conceptual obstacles in my
own path . . . Secretly, I have always realized my unlimited
passionateness, but no outlet seemed patterned or proper
enough—

I know now the capability of experiencing the greatest pleasure on a purely physical basis, sans "mental companionship," etc., although, of course, that is to be desired, too . . .

Irene came very close to ruining me—congealing the incipi-
ent guilt I have always felt about my lesbianism—making
me ugly to myself—

I know the truth now—I know how good and right it is to
love—I have, in some part, been given permission to live—

Everything begins from now—*I am reborn*


6/4/49

    Shostakovich Piano Concerto
    Scriabin Preludes
    Franck D Minor Symphony
    Prokofiev Symphony #5

    [Bach's] Mass in B Minor

Sex with music! So intellectual!!


6/6/49

I went out to Sausalito Saturday evening with H . . . Unless I
can drink I feel totally inane and awkward there . . . A and H
were together all the time . . . lots of ugly people were drinking and making themselves uglier, among them D . . . About
10:30 she and I went in[to] S[an] F[rancisco] together and I

really got drunk, as never before . . . I really couldn't take it a moment longer at the Tin Angel, and I knew H didn't care what I did . . . First we went to the 299, D's hangout, then to 12 Adler, where we met Bruce Boyd, and with him to a homosexual bar called the Red Lizard that was strictly something out of Walpurgisnacht, and then, naturally, ended up at the P.D. . . . D talked incessantly . . . she feels "evil" . . . "I'm from New England"

D (Ogunquit, ME.)

> "When I was 17 I wanted to find out what sex was
> so I went to a bar and picked up a sailor (he was a
> red head) and got raped, good and proper . . . Jesus!
> I couldn't sit down for weeks! And I was so afraid
> I was going to have a baby . . ."

marijuana

in a sanatorium for a while

"nervous breakdown"

measure success—"you don't know, you're young, you're still in school"—

season in summer stock as the business manager— Tin Angel—Navy?—Television job in N.Y. in fall

[. . .]

"I told you no lie—H—I'm fascinated by her"

•

We went back to her place, a room in the "Lincoln Hotel"—across the street from the Tin Angel—fell on the bed, and slept. The next afternoon she said she was now "regretting last night's wasted opportunity . . ."

I feel more depressed, drained than ever

Homosexual = gay

Heterosexual = jam (West Coast), straight (East)

*[Inserted on the next page]*

H.
c/o of M. Benjamin
305 West 69th Street
New York 23


6/11/49

H left for New York yesterday . . . I've been with Irene a great deal in the last week. God, does she have problems! I'm surprised that she's so honest with me . . . all this thinking and talking! . . . What people do to their lives, and *I don't want to be in love with limiting people* . . . Irene doesn't know how to cope with herself and her demands on herself . . . She talked about the "mediocrity" of her past life—she hasn't made good grades, etc.—an affair she had with a boy whom she recently learned is getting married . . . many people have betrayed her . . .

6/13/49

I want to think things through and sum up these five months, since in four days I'll be returning to Los Angeles [*e.g., to her mother and stepfather's home*] . . . Being with Irene so much recently has disrupted me a little . . . it's so effortless to let my loneliness defeat me, make me mold myself to whatever would (in some way—but not wholly) relieve it. *I am infinite*—I must never forget it . . . I want sensuality and sensitivity, both . . . I was more alive and satisfied with H than I have ever been with anyone else . . . Let me never deny that . . . I want to err on the side of violence and excess, rather than to underfill my moments . . .

6/19/49

. . . As if it had never been—

Yet the past is no more past because it was delimited within a particular geographic area from which one is now irrevocably departed, than if it were all lived in the same place . . .

But still, this miserable emptiness—as if I had never been away, as if these past five months had never existed, as if I had never known Irene and been in love with her, as if I had never discovered sex because of H, as if I had never discovered myself (did I?)—as if it had never been . . .

6/26/49

Time passes so slowly when there is an element of strangeness, of newness, in one's surroundings . . . It was thus during

my first weeks at Cal, and again, this past week—my first at
home—has been endless—


*[Undated, most likely early July 1949]*

There is no auditing at the UCLA summer session—I went
four days until I was ejected—The classes (with one exception: Meyerhoff's Philosophy 21) promised to be mediocre,
anyway—

I now have a Social Security card and a job as a file clerk at
Republic Indemnity Co. of America—Bob's office—at $125
a month, five days a week, beginning Monday—

I am reading [Oswald Spengler's] *The Decline of the West* . . .
Goethe's world. Conception, again . . . the Universal Plant. It
is very beautiful—

Some Goethe quoted in Spengler:

> *"What is important in life is life and not a result*
> *of life."*

> "Mankind? It is an abstraction. There are, always
> have been, and always will be, men and only men."
> (to Luden)

> . . .

> "Function, rightly understood, is existence consid-
> ered as an activity."

*[Undated, most likely mid or late July 1949.]*

. . . Idea for a story:

insurance office

personnel director—Jack Trater—bisexual—unhappy, poisoned by contempt + feelings of superiority—made a pass at Cliff—also Scott's sudden promotion from head of files (now Jack Paris' job) to underwriting—and Jack Paris now expects—

all office promotions depend on his good will

Terror.


6/29/49

Command: Read Gide's *New Fruits of the Earth.*

Again the anguished antithesis:

Myshkin:

> Motto: "stabo"—("I will stand firm")

> Albert Schweitzer's "reverence for life" is,
> satisfyingly articulated, just what I have always
> apprehended as the so-appealing essence of the
> Myshkine-Christian-Alyosha myth—love +
> pacifism—

So perfect and accessible a banner! A vision!
A justification and ennoblement of the pain one
would have been forced to endure anyway

Medea:

Motto: "Wolle die Wandlung"—Rilke ("Desire all
change")

Acceptance of my homosexuality—a rootless,
frantic life—make a drama of my unhappiness,
past, present, and future—give it design—
"rhythm, balance, unity in variety, and a cumulative
movement"

•

Keats:

"I am certain of nothing but the holiness of the
heart's affections and the truth of imagination"

"O for a life of sensations rather than of thoughts"

8/3/49

"Passion paralyzes good taste"

•

Can understand the whole thing. It would be so easy to
succumb:

A white-collar job in the day—clerical-typist book-keeper asst manager at Berlands

Bar at night

Lonely—wants sex

Anyone acceptable of the right sex, who is not ugly and will love + be faithful to me . . .

•

Gay slang:

gay
"a gay boy"
"a gay girl"
"the gay kids"

straight (east)
jam (west)
normal (tourist)

"he's straight"
"he's very jam"
"I lead a jam life"
"a jam friend of mine"
"I'm going normal"

"drag"

"be in drag"
"go in drag"
"a drag party"

Gay:

"86," "he 86'd me," "I was 86'd" (throw out,
[eject from a bar])

act "swishy," "I'm swish tonight" (effeminate)

"I'm fruit for——" (I'm crazy about——)

the "head," the "john" (toilet)

T.S. (tough shit)

"he's gay trade," "take it out in trade"
(one-night stands)

"go commercial," "I'm going commercial"
(for money)

"get a (have a) head on" (have an erection)

"a chippie" (a one-night-stand woman——
just for sex——no money)

"fall off the roof" (menstrual period) . . .

●

Patty: "are you for real," "I'll do until the real thing comes
along" real = gay

Negro "real ball" every year on So. Side of Chicago——people
from all over the country——around Hallowe'en

Negro——Hudson River Excursion trip——gay——annual . . .

●

Normal slang:

>"get a piece"
>"get a piece of tail" (have sex with a woman)
>
>"box" = vagina
>"have a box" = eat a woman
>("when you gonna let me have some of that box,
>honey?") . . .

•

Lord Byron:

>*Manfred* (incestuous passion for sister, Astarte)
>*Cain*
>*Don Juan*
>(was in love with his half-sister, Augusta Leigh)
>
>St. Hugh—Nov. 17
>St. David—patron saint of Wales

•

*[The rest of this notebook is devoted to detailed definitions,
comparisons, and illustrations of various poetic forms from
iambic pentameter to the six-line stanza.]*

8/5/49

With F last night. Said he + E had thought *a year ago* that
I was probably a lesbian. "Your only chance of being normal

[is] to call a halt right now. No more women, no more bars. You know that it will be the same thing in Chicago—in the dorm, in school, or in the gay bars . . . Go out with a couple of men at the same time. Park and let them feel you + have their little pleasures. You won't like it at all at first, but force yourself to do it . . . it's your only chance. And during that time don't see any women. If you don't stop now . . ."

•

1st m[ovement] Bach D Minor piano concerto
1st m[ovement] Bach E Major violin concerto
2nd m[ovement] Mozart Symphonie Concertante
2nd m[ovement] Beethoven [Piano] Trio opus 70a

*[Undated, August 1949]*

San Francisco: Mona's, Finocchio's, Paper Doll, The Black Cat, The Red Lizard, 12 Adler

New York: 181 Club—2nd Ave, 19th Hole—les, Jimmy Kelly's, Moroccan Village, San Remo's, Tony Pator's, Terry's, Mona's

Names of colors, animals

•

Proposed Gay Club: Beach House; hotel—rent a room, any time; bar—25¢ a drink; restaurant; two swimming pools

Near the beach

•

Books to buy:

Henry James: *Notebook[s]*, *The Ambassadors*,
*The Bostonians*, *Short Stories*, *Princess Casamassima*,
*Wings of the Dove*

Dostoyevsky: *The Idiot*, *A Raw Youth*, *Short Stories*

Conrad: *Portable*

Rilke: *Letters to a Young Poet*

Hesse: *Steppenwolf*

Fielding: *Joseph Andrews*, *Tom Jones*

Defoe: *Moll Flanders*

Gide: *New Fruits of the Earth*

A. S. Eddington: *The Nature of the Physical World*
(Macmillan—1929)

H. O. Taylor: *The Medieval Mind*

Dewey: *Art as Experience*

[Hart] Crane: [*Collected*] *Poems*

[Ernst] Cassirer: *Essay on Man*, *Language + Myth*


8/17/49

[M. E.] Gershenzon's argument in "A Correspondence Between Two Corners" expresses exactly what I have dumbly,
furtively, ashamedly felt in the past year; yet still it is a sub-
real, un-actualable conclusion, which will probably always
remain a semi-paralyzing potentiality.

Thus in still another reflection I find myself a foreigner.

Ich bin allein ["I am alone."]

Re-read "The Beast in the Jungle." An absolutely terrifying experience. I cannot dispel the immense depression in which it left me.

8/20/49

Read [André Gide's] *The Counterfeiters*. I am fascinated but not moved. I recall a childhood nightmare of an endlessly reflected image—a figure holding a mirror standing in front of another mirror, ad infinitum.

Here: a novel by Gide called *The Counterfeiters* dealing with a small chronological slice of life around a man called Edouard, who is planning to write a book called *The Counterfeiters*, but now is occupied with keeping a journal of his life while his life is colored by the *idea* of writing this book (as Hopkins sees the wreck of the *Deutschland* through a drop of Christ's blood)—and he thinks this journal will be more interesting than the proposed book, so that he now plans to publish the journal and never write the book. Edouard is Gide, beginning and ending in medias res.

8/26/49

I note with amusement my entrance into the anarchist-aesthete phase of my youth. I've read in succession during the last week: [I. A.] Richards' *Practical Criticism*, Koestler's *Darkness at Noon*, and the conclusion to [Walter] Pater's

*Renaissance.* I am sick of people, of stupidity and mediocrity, of crusades and politics . . .

•

e. e. cummings:

> *"down they forgot as up they grew"*

8/30/49

I have neatly neglected to describe this summer's non-intellectual (!) activities until now: the moment of their denouement. I was never as conscious of their stature until I told Peter the whole story when he came back last week. My second affair—imagine! . . . Yet the only tangible good I probably have gotten out of the summer is my closeness to E, whose intelligence I genuinely respect. How different it all was from the severe regimen I prescribed for myself before I came back from Berkeley. There would be no sex for the summer, thought I! And how completely antithetical H and L are! All *very* humorous!

I said good-bye to L tonight. Sex again, of course. I discover in myself an irradicable and very dangerous streak of tenderness—without logical substantiation, even in opposition to all reason, I recognize that I have been moved by L, feeling more than a rational acceptance of the physical and egotistical gratification she has given me . . . Yet when I think what H would have done, were she in a comparable position! Though I admire ruthlessness and arrogance, I cannot wholly despise my own weakness . . .

8/31/49

p. 226—[Samuel Butler's] *The Way of All Flesh*—Mrs. Jupp uses the word "gay" to describe a promiscuous woman—

"she is gay"

"a gay woman"

9/1/49

My intellectual dislike of the physical passivity of a woman in heterosexual relationships was, I see now, just an attempt to find a reason for not being attracted to that kind of sex . . . For after being "femme" to H and "butch" to L, I recall finding greater physical satisfaction in being "passive," though emotionally I am definitely the lover type, not the beloved . . . (God, how absurd this all is!!)

•

La Rochefoucauld (1613–1680):

> "We have all sufficient strength to support the pain
> of others."

9/2/49

Left Los Angeles at 1:30 p.m.

Impossible to comprehend . . .

9/3/49

On the train: Arizona, New Mexico:

Fairy-tale coloring in the dry river beds—(very wide [20–30 ft.] and 4–5 ft. deep)—smooth, rivuleted rose-colored sand, and on the miniature cliffs banking the bed are little silvery-green shrubs—

9/4/49

Arrived in Chicago at 7:15 a.m.

This is the ugliest city I've ever seen: one continuous slum . . . The downtown district—refuse-littered, narrow streets, the noise of the El, the perpetual darkness and smell, the swaying tattered old men, the penny arcades, the "Photostat" joints, the movie-houses—*Love in a Nudist Colony*—*Tells All*—*The Naked Truth*—*Uncut.*

•

In a bookstore on State St. I thumbed through two volumes of [Wilhelm] Stekel: *The Homosexual Neurosis* and *Bisexual Love*—He believes that humans are naturally *bisexual*—the Greeks have been the only culture to recognize this . . .

9/5/49

Arrived in New York at 8:45 a.m.

9/8/49

I've made my annual obeisances to Uncle Aaron and been granted the $722 for my room and board this year . . . I am, then, completely secure financially . . .

9/12/49

Three oases in a desert of relatives and moral blackmail:

*Death of a Salesman* [Arthur Miller]

*Le Diable au corps* [film of the novel by Raymond Radiguet]

*The Silver Tassie* [play by Sean O'Casey]

*[SS inserted the* Playbills *for the Miller and the O'Casey into the notebook.]*

The Arthur Miller play was very powerful—magnificent set by Jo Mielziner beautifully acted and directed—it's just not really *written* . . .

The Radiguet film [starring] Gérard Philipe was sensitive in every way though it did not have the classic stature of a "Symphonie Pastorale" . . .

The O'Casey play was given a good, but definitely surpassable performance . . . It is a puzzling work, and not too successful, I think, although moments of it are magnificent, and the first act is sustainedly moving and beautiful . . . The symbolic second act was not wholly integrated with the realism of the first . . . and the frank, ingenuous pity for the hero in the last two acts is an anticlimax after the excitingly complex attitudes of the first two acts . . .


9/15/49

*The Madwoman of Chaillot.* The most beautiful theatre I've seen here. It was pure, infinitely contoured spectacle. Her walk, her hands, her gestures! Their precision made me ache with empathically reversed gracelessness . . .

•

Greek collection at the Met[ropolitan Museum of Art]:

> Marble statue of an *Old Market Woman*—2nd Cent. B.C. Leaning forward, *looking*, mouth slack. [*This entry is followed by a sketch of the statue.*]

[*The following entry is crossed out.*] Look back on the 16 years. [*SS would not turn seventeen until January of the following year.*] A *good* beginning. Could be better: more erudition, definitely, but it's unreasonable to expect much more emotional maturity than I have at this point . . . Everything is in my favor, my early emancipation, my [*Entry ends here.*]

•

How much of homosexuality is narcissism?

•

Revulsion: Maybe Gide is right: separation of love and passion (c.f., Introduction to M[odern] L[ibrary] edition of *The Counterfeiters*).

•

(I read dutifully, obediently, plastically! . . .)

•

Pacemakers:

Cézanne:

> *Vase of Tulips*—1890–4
> (greens)
>
> *Mont Sainte-Victoire*—1900
> (blue, *white*, yellow, pink)

•

Still this childish fascination with my handwriting . . . To think that I always have this sensuous potentiality glowing within my fingers!

9/27/49

. . . How to defend the aesthetic experience? More than pleasure, because you cannot evaluate works of art by the *amount* of pleasure it gives—but that *it itself* is better—No, this is illogical . . .

•

. . . How do mental operations exist?

•

. . . Beethoven quartet vs. Euclid theorem

•

need for order

•

*[All her life, SS made lists of words into which she occasionally inserted a person's name or a brief observation. This undated, fall 1949 entry is representative and shows how early this habit became second nature for her.]*

effete
noctambulous
perfervid
detumescence
disheveled
so alluring, so cerebral
sodden
intriguing
corrupt dignity
lotophagous
elegiac
Meleager
disponibility
pardine
demotic
Harriette Wilson
garbure
satura
succulent

competent intellectual vulgarity of Aldous Huxley
*Yellow Book* preciousness
secretive
sturdy
pedantry + lechery
spleen
ribaldry
ilex
Klaxon

•

[*The*] *Rock Pool*—Cyril Connolly, p. 213

". . . so perhaps don't we all try unconsciously to
preserve the plumage in which people have
first found us desirable."

•

10/21/49

I returned to Chicago, without joy, + to find not only the
anticipated grimness, but a new trial. Again, my lack of
practical knowledge has subjected me to a genuine, + almost
defeating, ordeal. These last few weeks have been vitally
revealing in the same way as my summer employment of a
year ago. I learned then that I cannot endure white-collar
work, + that I could not count on being able to get along
after college, reading, *writing*, etc., and with any job to
give me enough money to live. (I had naïvely supposed that
it was better to do something meaningless than something

pseudo-intellectual, i.e., teaching—I did not realize how apathetic, *drained* one becomes by the activity of most of one's working hours.) That eliminated one-half of my aspirations toward proletarian living, + my present manner of physical existence has stripped off the other half of my illusion!

•

*J'Accuse* last night. But one feels the horror, and despairs, *only* if one already knows!

(A thought on Peter's terrible poetry: Lack of technique, as he said? No. Lack of taste. I feel nothing but contempt for his personality, abilities, + beliefs!)

*Himlaspelet*: brilliantly mature *technically* (i.e., sensuously), naïve *ethically* (spiritually); *Der Müde Tod* gross + naïve technically, mature ethically. Which of the two would I rather see again? *Himlaspelet*. Because it has more "art"?

My relation with E has melted—

Such unstruggling emptiness of his life . . .

A new subject, a new world—the philosophy of history. Bossuet, Condorcet, Herder, Ranke, Burkhardt, Cassirer—

Re-read: [André Gide's] *The Immoralist*. The next books I want to read are the Kafka diaries.

11/21/49

Excellently staged performance of *Don Giovanni* last night (City Center). Today, a wonderful opportunity was offered me—to *do* some research work for a soc[iology] instructor named Philip Rieff, who is working on, among other things, a reader in the sociology of politics + religion. At last the chance to really involve myself in one area with competent guidance.

12/2/49

*[SS and PR were in fact married on this date in 1950.]*

Last night, or was it early this (Sat.) morning?—I am engaged to Philip Rieff. [*Next to this entry, in the margin, SS notes: "Jennie Tourel* Das Marienleben."]

12/13/49

Morality informs experience, not the reverse. I am my history, yet in my moral desire to understand my past, to be fully self-conscious I become precisely what my history demonstrates that I am not—free.

12/28/49

*[In this notebook, which has entries going all the way to early 1951, and includes SS's narration of her visit to Thomas Mann—an event she would write about many years later in a memoir (one of the few she ever undertook)—there is an epigraph from Bacon on the first page that reads: "Whatever his*

*mind seizes and dwells upon with peculiar satisfaction is to be held in suspicion."]*

E, F, and I interrogated God this evening at six [*in the margin, SS has noted Thomas Mann's phone number*]. We sat, immobilized with awe, outside his house (1550 San Remo Drive) from 5:30 to 5:55, rehearsing. His wife, slight, grey face and hair, opened the door. He at the far end of the large living room on the couch, holding a large black dog by the collar, which we'd heard barking as we had approached. Beige suit, maroon tie, white shoes—feet together, knees apart—(Bashan!)—Very controlled, undistinguished face, exactly like his photographs. He led us into his study (walls lined with book-cases, of course)—his speech is slow and precise, and his accent is much less prominent than I expected—"But—O tell us what the oracle said"—

On *The Magic Mountain*:

> Was begun before 1914, and finished, after many interruptions, in 1934—

> "a pedagogical experiment"

> "allegorical"

> "like all German novels, it is an education novel"

> "I tried to make a summa of all the problems facing Europe before World War I"

> "It's to ask questions, not to give solutions—that would be too presumptuous"

"Didn't you feel it was humanely written—that there was optimism in it? It's not a nihilistic book. It was written with benevolence and good will"

"Hans Castorp represents the generation that was to rebuild the world after the War to freedom, peace, and democracy"

"Settembrini is the humanist; he represents the Western world"

"treacherous"

[*SS*]: All the temptations—influences—to which Hans is exposed—important to realize that (and how) Hans knows more when he goes down than before—is more mature—conjuring up of Joachim.

[*Mann continues*]: "This relates to a personal experience of mine in Munich before the War—I still to this day don't know whether it was reality or not—'meta-psychological' "

*[Above the page setting down the last of these comments by Mann, SS writes: "The author's comments betray his book with their banality."]*

His [*e.g., Mann's*] works form a unity and preferably should be analyzed as a whole—(*Buddenbrooks* to [*Doctor*] *Faustus*)—[*Mann*]: "In the literary life ideas are related and continuous"—

Translations:

"The best translation of *The M[agic] M[ountain]* is
by a French poet, Maurice Betz, who also translated
the poems of Rilke with great delicacy."

The best "Englishing" of any work of his is
Kenneth Burke's *Death in Venice*—

"My publisher, Alfred Knopf, has a pious faith in
Mrs. Lowe's ability to translate me—of course,
she knows my work very well."

*Faustus* was a very difficult book to translate.
[*Mann*]: "It has one foot in the sixteenth century"
because of the old High (Lutheran) German—

On contemporary writers:

Joyce:

1.  was uncertain as to the *Portrait*'s [*e.g.*, A Portrait
    of the Artist as a Young Man] place in Joyce's
    order of composition (his second book?)

2.  difficult for one not born into the English-
    speaking "culture" to appreciate the beauty

3.  has read books *on* Joyce

4.  believed there is a similarity between Joyce and
    himself:—the place of myth in their works
    (*Ulysses, Joseph* [*and his Brothers*], *The M[agic]
    M[ountain]*)

5. thinks Joyce is "one of the most important
   writers of our time"

Proust:

Both Proust and himself have the emphasis on time, but
Mann became acquainted with Proust long after *The
M[agic] M[ountain]*—"Time is a contemporary problem."

On [*Doctor*] *Faustus*:

"It is a Nietzsche-book"—begun in 1942, finished
in 1946

Collaboration on the musical part with a pupil of Alban Berg
named Darnoldi—also was seeing and talking with Schoenberg a great deal during the time of the writing of the
book—used Schoenberg's *Harmonielehre*—

He is presently working on a fairly short "narrative"—not
a full length novel—will be about three hundred pages—
hopes to finish it by April—is "mythical," "fairy tale,"
"tragic-comical." Taken from a poem by the German minne-
singer [medieval troubadour], Hartmann von Aue—"It is the
story of a great sinner"—but "who was free from guilt"—
"a pious, grotesque tale"

[*Mann's account of the plot*]: Son of incestuous union
(brother-sister) is cast away from home—mountain? Ocean?
Returns in manhood, marries his mother—ends by becoming pope—this will be even harder than *Faustus* to translate—contains a mixture of Old German, Middle German,
Old English, Old French

New Swiss book—on how *Faustus* was written—the writing
was interrupted by a lung operation—won't be translated—

[*Mann*]: "Just an intimate little book for friends"—"people
might think too 'conceited' "

[*Next to this page, SS has written*]: Digression: Apology for
unsatisfactory answers to the questions—1. Poor knowledge
of English 2. Difficulty of questions (*M*[*agic*] *M*[*ountain*]
will be 25 years—a silver jubilee—"a rather important
jubilee")

12/29/49

Finished re-reading the Joyce, *Portrait*—

Oh, the ecstasy of aloneness!— . . .

12/31/49

Today: two [Frank Lloyd] Wright houses (Aztec period) and
[Handel's] *The Messiah* afterwards at the Rhapsody.

A new year! But no crap on this occasion . . .

# 1950

1/3/50

*[This entry was in fact written on this date in 1951.]*

I marry Philip with full consciousness + fear of my will toward self-destructiveness.

1/5/50

*[SS has returned to Chicago and the college spring term.]*

An enervating train trip, and "as if it had never been." This quarter promises to be more stimulating academically. Schwab is as magnificent as ever (he's giving a seminar in Moral Science at the Baptist Church every other Sunday in which E and I are enrolled!)—and two professors in English audits, R. S. Crane and Elder Olson, are unbelievably superior and illuminating. I'm enrolled in Maynard Kruger's soc[iology] class, too (economic this quarter), but I won't go until the third week. E. K. Brown is doing a very competent job on [Jane Austen's] *Pride and Prejudice* in the same hour.

And [Kenneth] Burke, of course, for whom I must write a paper on [Conrad's] *Victory* . . .

1/9/50

Re-read:

*Doctor Faustus*

Read:

Antonia White, *Frost in May*

Aldous Huxley, *Eyeless in Gaza*

Herbert Read, *The Green Child*

Henry James, [*The*] *Portrait of a Lady*

1/16/50

*[SS's seventeenth birthday; this is the sole entry for this date.]*

Marcellus I was the successor of Marcellinus—assumed the pontificate in May 308 under Maxentius; was banished from Rome in 308 on account of the tumult caused by the severity of the penances he had imposed on Christians who had lapsed under the recent persecution; died in the same year + was succeeded by Eusebius.

1/25/50

I am reading *War + Peace*, *The Journal of a Disappointed Man* (Barbellion), + the Apocryphal New Testament, and meditating on holy dying.

2/13/50

*[This entry was in fact written on this date in 1951.]*

*War + Peace* is an incomparable experience; also reading in Christopher Caudwell: *Illusion + Reality*, Ernst Troeltsch, [Robert] Murray, *The Political Consequences of the Reformation*, Rilke letters, Dewey on logic, + the [Edward] Carr biography of Dostoyevsky.

From Rilke:

> ". . . the great question-dynasty: . . . if we are
> continually inadequate in love, uncertain in
> decision, + impotent in the face of death, how
> is it possible to exist?"

Yet we do exist, + affirm that. We affirm the life of lust. Yet there *is* more. One flees not from one's real nature which is animal, id, to a self-torturing externally imposed conscience, super-ego, as Freud would have it—but the reverse, as Kierkegaard says. Our ethical sensitivity is what is natural to man + we flee from it to the beast; which is merely to say that I reject weak, manipulative, despairing lust, I am not a beast, I will not to be a futilitarian. I believe in more than the personal epic with the hero-thread, in more than my own life: above multiple spuriousness + despair, there is freedom + transcendence. One *can* know worlds one has not experienced, choose a response to life that has *never been* offered, create an inwardness utterly strong + fruitful.

But how, when one can, to instrument the fact of wholeness + love? One must attempt more than the surety of reflexive nurturing. If "life is a hollow form, a negative mold, all the grooves + indentations of which are agony, disconsolations + the most painful insights, then the casting from this . . . is happiness, assent—most perfect + most certain bliss." But how protected + resolved one would have to be! And this leads one outside art to the dying, the madness—oh, where is the *out-going* freedom, the instrumental freedom from, freedom that is not *this enormous possession of one's own heart which is death?*

The war is so close. We have reservations on the *Queen Elizabeth* for June 22nd.


*[Undated, most likely late February 1950.]*

Balzac—"In the Time of the Terror"—

Her face was "like the face of a person who practices austerities in secret."

> Enid Welsford: *The Fool*
> (Faber + Faber, London, 1935)

> M. Willson Disher: *Clowns + Pantomimes*
> (London, 1925)

G. Kitchin, [*A Survey of*] *Burlesque* + *Parody in English*

Empson: *English Pastoral Poetry*
(Norton + Co, NY, 1938)

[Kenneth] Burke, *Permanence* + *Change*
            *Attitudes Toward History*

*Art* + *Scholasticism*—Maritain
[*On*] *Growth* + *Form*—D'Arcy W. Thompson
*Moral Values* + *the Moral Life*—[Etienne] Gilson
*The Mind of Primitive Man*—Boas

*Lost Treasures of Europe* (Pantheon)

Seebohm: *The Oxford Reformers*
St. John of the Cross: *The Ascent of Mount Carmel*
Jacob Boehme: *Aurora*
Meister Eckhart: *Sermons*
Traherne: *Centuries of Meditations*

Lynn Thorndike [*A*] *History of Magic and Experimental Science*

H. Malter: *Saadia Gaon*
E. R. Bevan + C. Singer: *The Legacy of Israel*
I. Husik: [*A*] *History of Mediaeval Jewish Philosophy*
Leon Roth: *Spinoza, Descartes,* + *Maimonides*
S. Schechter: *Studies in Judaism*
S. Zeitlin: *Maimonides*

Desert + flashes melted together in a mirror—[*A*] *Passion in the Desert* (Balzac)

Quis—who
Quid—what
Ubi—where, when
Quibis auxiliis—by the aid of what
Quia—why
Quo modo—in what manner
Quando—how

*[The first page of this entry is missing, but it was certainly written in the first ten days of September 1950.]*

I spent last weekend in Balboa with Sophia and Petie, and retook my BiSci comp. Talking with Sophia, not about myself specifically, nevertheless was very enlightening, as usual.

I asked how one discusses death with a young child, +, another evening, about the dichotomy between sex and affection. Self-applications:

1. The most reasonable answer to my current neurotic anxiety about death: it is annihilation— everything (organism, event, thought, etc.) has form, has a beginning and an end—death is as natural as birth—nothing lasts forever nor would we want to—Once we are dead, we don't know about it, so think of being alive! Even if we die before experiencing things we demand from life, it won't matter when we die—we lose only the moment we are "in"—life is horizontal, not vertical—*it cannot be accumulated* so live, don't grovel.

2. It is impossible to disassociate satisfactory sex from affection—impossible, that is, for me—although I have thought that I was—The two are irrevocably associated in my mind, otherwise I would not have rejected sexual experiences so often—Sex has been a secret, silent, dark admission of affectional need, which must be forgotten when vertical—Let me remember this!

3. My need to "confess" to Mother was not commendable at all—it does not show me to be upright and honest but 1) weak, seeking to strength[en] the only affectional relationship I have, + 2) sadistic—since my illicit activities are an expression of rebellion; they are not efficacious unless known!

9/11/50

Re-read: *Brave New World*

Read: "Chance"—unforced, clear structure but dubious resolution; marvelously elaborate analysis of motives—

11/4/50

*[It is not clear what poem SS is referring to.]*

No, I don't like the poem at all! It is crowded, confused ethically—quite tastelessly complicated. But it is "good" not "artistically" but "historically"—as growing from the passionate acceptance of solitude, which I have so longed for. I embrace my solitude as a beautiful gift; I will become beautiful through it!

11/5/50

"His face was one of those which, for fear of misuse, has not been used at all." ([Djuna] Barnes)

11/6/50

[Edward "Ned"] Rosenheim told me today that [Kenneth] Burke said that mine was the best of all the preceptorial papers—that means better than E's! If I could only convince myself that he is not so innately superior to me, I would not be constantly disturbed by the thought of his life and actions, passive, without integrity and his lack of the knowledge only to [be] acquired through extensive + careful reading in philosophy, history, + literature. He is indifferent to these things, toward which I wholly burn: morality, creation, chaos, knowledge, sensuality; yet I am terrified by the idea that he has a *natural* ability + competence which I shall never have!

11/12/50

I found out more of what happened to my *Nightwood* paper: After it was read by Burke (who called it a "stunner" in his letter to Rosenheim), it was given to the other reader, some Humanities instructor who didn't like it at all. Burke's opinion being so weighty, an exception was made + a third reader, another Humanities instructor was asked to read it and arbitrate. He liked it even less! Finally the Humanities staff called on Wallace Fowlie, who happened to be on campus at the time, + his decision was to be final. Fowlie liked the paper as much as Burke! (I looked up what Fowlie has to say about the book in one [of] his critical volumes (*The Clown's Grail*) yesterday—his p[oint] o[f] v[iew] is religious (Catholic?), but the analysis seemed much more cogent than Frank's.

I'm reading [Jack London's novel] *Martin Eden* for the first time in three years. I can see clearly now, over four years after I first read it, how enormous a personal influence it has been on me, despite the fact that I consider it insignificant as art. Although I had read adult literature as a child (*Twenty Thousand Years in Sing Sing*, *Heavenly Discourse*, *Les Misérables*, + the Lamb [*Tales from Shakespeare*] I remember all before the age of nine!), the reading of the London book coincided with my real awakening to life, as marked by my beginning these notebooks at the end of my twelfth year. There is not an idea in *Martin Eden* about which I do not have a strong conviction, and many of my conceptions were formed under the direct stimulus of this novel—my atheism + the value I place on physical energy + its expression, creativity, sleep and death, and the possibility of happiness! . . .

For many persons, the "awakening" book is at the same time a great affirmation—like Joyce's *Portrait*—so that their adolescence is full of hopeful passion, + only later in adulthood do they encounter disillusion. But for me, the "awakening" book preached despair + defeat, and I have grown up literally never daring to expect happiness . . .

And Martin's "trick of visioning"—London's vulgar panoramic flash-back device—by which, in every important moment of his life, he is confronted with a pageant of his past—This has been a necessity for me for the last four years: to document + structure my experiences, to understand my growth as dialectic—to be fully conscious at every moment which means feeling the past to be as real as the present— For the first time I see the source of this mode of life, of these narcissistic concerns, in this book . . . Hopeful passion exists in virtue of the external desire + the striving towards it; the despairing passionateness which I from the first adopted has only a reflective nurturing—it feeds on itself— the only good it can attain is knowledge . . . An even more ignoble consequence of this type of pessimism is in one's social behavior—One becomes an intellectual vampire! . . .

11/17/50

Re-read: another crucial "early" book for me—[Maugham's] *The Summing Up*—at 13 to be wholly converted to such an urbane aristocratic stoicism! And the structure of his literary taste of course has greatly influenced me—and, above all, again, *the pattern.*

•

*[N.B. I found no other entries for 1950 and no notebook for 1952 among SS's effects after her death. Whether she kept no diaries during these two years, got rid of those she kept, or if they were lost I do not know.]*

# 1953

1/19/53

In Schoenhof's [*bookstore in Cambridge, Mass.*] today—waiting, nauseated again, for Philip to choose a book for [Professor Aron] Gurwitsch's birthday, after the Descartes *Correspondance* is discovered épuisé—I opened a volume of Kafka short stories; at a page of "[The] Metamorphosis." It was like a physical blow, the *absoluteness* of his prose, pure actuality *nothing* forced or obscure. How I admire him above all other writers! Beside him, Joyce is so stupid, Gide so—yes—sweet, Mann so hollow + bombastic. Only Proust is as interesting—almost. But Kafka has that magic of actuality in even the most dislocated phrase that no other modern has, a kind of shiver + grinding blue ache in your teeth. As in [Robert Browning's] "Childe Roland to the Dark Tower Came"—so certain pages in the Kafka diaries, phrases—"But they cannot; all things possible do happen, only what happens is possible."

•

That quality of openness—terrifying—unforced writing that is the highest genius. Tolstoy had it above all, + the lack of it makes almost all modern writing that is really talented so minor, like [Nathanael West's] *Miss Lonelyhearts* or *Nightwood.*

1/21/53

Enormously depressed, silenced, by a sequence of dreams over the past weeks, reaching an unbelievably real climax last night. Their subject? But, of course, what else! Philip set the alarm for 5:00 a.m., which I heard. I wanted to get up. But I knew that if I consented to fall back I would have my reward. Asleep, it began again—only this time agonizingly real. I could just reach out . . .

There was a kind of cliff leading down to a pier, later a room with a three-quarter bed of very dark wood, and still later the stage of an auditorium.

I said: "I'll give you all the money you want." But earlier on the pier, I had said, "Of course, you can have any money you want, but you won't need it or want it. It isn't good for you." The second time I was begging, whereas before I was so confident, almost patronizing . . .

When I stepped into the room + saw the bed, I knew it wasn't a bed in which one slept alone.

You live with someone, I shouted. Then he stepped from behind the door, I think, and he was very old. I remember 67, that age precisely, small, stiff short grey hair. "I live with him because he is rich."

I stood at the side of the stage, in some kind of ceremonial dress. A great crowd awaited me, but still I dared carelessly to touch the side of my hand to hers . . .

These excruciating pleasures—completion + sadness—are like nothing outside a dream. The fact that I had bought this pleasure did not lessen its completeness. Being inexplicably regal, I could expect no more, and flesh was still flesh, purchased or not. I ask only to weep for a very long time, to be properly comforted, to refuse all comfort. I could cry for three days, perhaps, scream and sob without apologizing for my dripping nose. But I don't, because then I would have to do something afterwards, not sink back. That is, kill myself or leave.

Barring these two actions, I dare not weep, only the smallest time . . .

That dream, and the others before, pile up in my head like an enormously heavy soggy lump—pushing my head into my stomach, burdening me with nauseated, melodramatic silences . . .

Philip even thinks I am sick, my poor dearest. While I struggle to be one—to set my heart under my hand—my hair decides to thin out as I comb it, and though I plead with him, he has made an appointment with the doctor . . .

1/22/53

What makes prose "absolute" is often a kind of intellectual swiftness—but it must be borne very lightly, only emerging within concrete perceptions. It's this quality that makes *Un*

*Crime* so good, although the rest of [Georges] Bernanos is lousy. The bat swings upside down in the mind of the inspector, who has a cold and tosses feverishly in his dirty hotel room.

Prose everywhere.

Compact + expressive + swift.

Really, it is style that is the important thing. The style selects the plot.

From now on—as discipline—I will avoid dialogue as much as possible, since in my stories so far, it is almost all dialogue— + very bad too—but nothing in between.

Thus: The professor called a meeting at his home on a Sunday evening for the junior members of his department. He wanted to silence the accelerating rumors which concerned one young instructor who, it was said, was not to be rehired next year. This instructor was not present, etc.

# 1954

anaesthesia as the model of virtue (connection with power)


8/17/54

Tonight (2:30 a.m., home from the room, hungry, red-eyed, sleepy), I prepared a bowl of pineapple to eat when P urged me to add some cottage cheese to it; he got the partly full container from the ice-box + began to scoop the entire contents into my plate. I said (+ though I meant it), "Don't, I only want part," took the spoon from him, + to my own amazement, scooped all the cheese into the plate myself.

Suddenly I understood why David can vehemently refuse something + at the same time accept it. For the child, life is so utterly self-centered that there is no impulse to be consistent, which is already a limitation on desire.

·

The problem of influence (communication, on the highest intellectual level) seems to indicate that one's thought is much more innerly detachable (separable) than any great mind wants to admit. The study of the influence of any mind is a natural corrective to his own systematizing presumptions, his own insistence on inessentials of belief.

Need a vocabulary with which to discuss influences. Have now only the notion of orthodoxy, disciples, heretics (on religious model) to discuss great intellectual movements like Freudianism or Marxism; need words to pin down the more loosely influenced.

Might involve ranking concepts themselves. Those of 1st importance [*in the margin SS writes: "But how to define 'importance'?"*], second, third, etc. Then rank circles of influence around a centrifuge of dogmatism + a centripetal pull of "partial incorporation."

Thus one may be Freudian without believing in the Primal Crime, Lamarckianism, the dirty reason, etc., by the tyranny of psychologizing itself—e.g., explaining Veblen's positive image of primitivity (wasteful, feckless, whimsical, easygoing) as a / by a preference for his mother (with same qualities) over his truculent father whom he feared + with whom he always feared to compete.

What is Freudian here is the family psychologizing; what is more general than Freud [*in the margin, SS writes: "Don't lay all this on Freud's head"*] is the assumption that intellectual decisions only confirm (enact) subjective (irrational) preferences

# 1955

4/8/55

Reception by [*what would later turn out to be the CIA-underwritten*] Committee on Cultural Freedom for leader of Australian Conservative Party, Mr. Wentworth: a reddish, short, smiling political-looking man in his late fifties; his hands are in his pockets; his teeth are prominent; his toes point outward; he has a bird-like cock of the head, offensively attentive, confident, smiling. He spoke of the death of cities, of the exigencies of survival . . .

*[The following entries are undated, but were written sometime in April 1955.]*

Why we [*e.g., SS and PR*] don't need a Dictaphone—missing the incentive of making erotic gift of one's intellect (not the inhibition of the machine + the trouble to turn it on, etc.).

This is why speech is so much easier + more copious compared to the labor of keeping a journal + the pathetic paucity of the entries over months of time as compared to all that one says in a single evening.

Journal ([Stéphane] Mallarmé's blank page) is inhibiting; speech is de-inhibiting because journal is narcissistic + speech is social + erotic + has more incentive in the feared + desired expectations of the other than in the perfectly knowable + less mysterious + compelling self demands.

•

Early example of *collage*

John Frederick Peto (1854–1907): called *Ordinary Objects in the Artist's Creative Mind* (oil on canvas)

# 1956

1/15/56

"Jewish Gnosticism"—[Gershom] Scholem

Reitzenstein's theories of the Iranian origin of Gnosticism—very influential, now thought to be speculative

Now [it] is held that Christian Gnosticism was preceded by a "Jewish" Gnosticism

Newly discovered (18 yrs. Ago) Gnostic papyri at Nag Hammadi—13 codices

"Gospel of Truth," etc.

Here is expounded a monotheistic (non-dualistic) form of Valentinian Gnosticism—preceding the dualistic antinomian teaching the Church Fathers talk about . . .

8/12/56

Has the "spirit" power? Was one of the main themes in the philosophy of the late Max Scheler; and the only answer he

could find was "yes," but only through the *non-frat,* of veto-
ing the course of events + delaying the chain of brutal actions

·

In marriage, every desire becomes a decision

9/3/56

All aesthetic judgment is really cultural evaluation

    (1) Koestler example—pearls / milkdrops
    (2) "fakes"

·

9/4/56

The beloved egoism of children . . .

college instruction is a brand of popular culture; the univer-
sities are poorly run mass media

Whoever invented marriage was an ingenious tormentor. It
is an institution *committed* to the dulling of the feelings. The
whole point of marriage is repetition. The best it aims for is
the creation of strong, mutual dependencies.

Quarrels eventually become pointless, unless one is always
prepared to act on them— that is, to end the marriage. So,
after the first year, one stops "making up" after quarrels—
one just relapses into angry silence, which passes into ordinary silence, and then one resumes again.

10/20/56

. . . Tolstoy's *War and Peace*

basic theme: survival of an anti-heroic epic

Kutuzov, the anti-hero on the national scale, triumphs over the hero, Napoleon

Pierre, the anti-hero on the individual scale, prevails over the hero, Andrey

10/23/56

6:30, Philosophy Club dinner, with M[argaret]-M[asterman] Braithwaite

at 8:00, her talk: "Towards a Logical Definition of Meta-physics" (Emerson B)

Spinoza—the greatest metaphysician.

[Harvard philosopher Willard Van Orman] Quine moving toward view of a total body of statements—so the problem doesn't arise about some being verifiable + others not.

10/24/56

To philosophize, or to be a culture-conserver? I had never thought of being anything other than the latter . . .

Thought has no *natural* boundaries.

Philosophy is topology of thought . . .

Project: to make a scheme or chart of philosophic moves (ploys). Philosophy as a game. (Learn chess!) For [nineteenth-century American chess master] Paul Morphy to play chess well doesn't help me much to play well. (It helps a little.) Hence philosophy is done over and over

In philosophy the snake swallows its tail; thinking, about thinking[2]—two senses of "thinking." Thinking is philosophy; thinking[2] = the sciences.

But architectural or aesthetic (or logical—same thing!) considerations can't be *all* that determines the election of one philosophic system over another. In that case there would be no true + false metaphysics.

"Allow me to X-ray your argument . . ."

"Allow me to unravel your system . . ."

"Pardon me while I excavate your motives . . ."

In philosophy you probe, tenderly, the boundaries of thought—or you shove at them—or you pull them in, towards you—or you spit at them—or you paint beautiful friezes around them.

What is thinking without words? If you try it, you can't. Thinking strains to *be* words, perversely, (see [British neurologist John] Hughlings Jackson's notion of "internal speech")

Words are the coins of thought, but they are not the cash-value of thought. (This contra the linguistic philosophers at Oxford)

10/31/56

The world is a unique object.—it is in this sense that it has
no boundary.

The three philosophers I admire most, Plato Nietzsche
Wittgenstein, were avowedly anti-systemizers. Could it be
shown that the arch-systemizer—the philosopher who thrust
his own noble spirit hardest down on the Procrustean bed—
I mean Spinoza—is best understood if his system is unrav-
eled and interpreted *aphoristically*? [*In the margin, SS writes
"contra Wolfson."*] (S[øren] K[ierkegaard] was certainly right
about Hegel.)

Solipsism is the only *true* philosophy, if philosophy is to
mean something different from common sense. But, of
course, it doesn't and isn't. So we are not looking for a *true*
philosophy.

11/1/56

All day, David wants to know, "*When* do you die in your
sleep" (after I recited the bedtime prayer, Now I lay me . . . ,
to him this morning).

We've been discussing the soul.

11/3/56

Today I explained to him [*David*] about hell—when he said,
"Don Giovanni dies, doesn't he?"

Later I heard this:

> David: Ro' [*Rose McNulty, SS's nanny and then*
> *DR's*], do you know about El, where bad
> people go?
> Rose: Uh.
> David: Do you [know] about Don Giovanni?
> He killed the Old Commander, but the
> Old Commander came back—he still
> had his strength (i.e., his soul)— + put
> Don Giovanni down in El.
> Rose: Uh.

•

Is the *philosophy* of religion possible? Doesn't it "empty out" its subject-matter? What can "*religion*" mean, outside of concrete historical religions?

Pascal: To reject philosophy is already to philosophize.

11/4/56

Hungary on the slaughter-bench of history . . . [*The refer-ence is to Hegel's phrase "History is a slaughter-bench."*]

On Tuesday, in the first Israeli tank entering the Sinai Peninsula the Grand Rabbi placed a Torah, saying, "You are entering holy land. This is where Moses gave our fathers the law."

•

Concerning the death of Gertrude Stein: she came out of a deep coma to ask her companion Alice Toklas, "Alice, Alice, what is the answer?" Her companion replied, "There is no answer." Gertrude Stein continued, "Well, then, what is the question?" and fell back dead.

11/16/56

Henry James

The bachelor life was precisely the medium through which James practiced his spectatorship.

Read Miss [Theodora] Bosanquet's *Memoirs* [*Henry James at Work*]—James' typist in later years. Leon Edel says the break between the "middle" + "late" (gaseous) style comes just at the point when James stopped dictating to a secretary who took shorthand + started dictating to Miss B. who typed as he spoke. A Remington was the only typewriter whose rhythms he could bear, + on his deathbed—at his last moments—he called for his Remington. And she typed for him. James died to the tune of his typewriter.

Flaubert would have appreciated this—pathos of the artist's vocation.

11/18/56

A Project—Notes on Marriage

Marriage is based on the principle of *inertia*.

Unloving proximity.

Marriage is all private—no public—behavior.

The glass wall that separates one couple from another.

Friendship in marriage. The smooth skin of the other.

[Protestant theologian Paul] Tillich: the marriage vow is idolatric (places one moment above all others, gives that moment [the] right to determine all the future ones). Monogamy, too. He spoke disparagingly of the "extreme monogamy" of the Jews.

Rilke thought the only way to keep love in marriage was by perpetual acts of separation–return.

The leakage of talk in marriage.
(My marriage, anyway.)


12/1/56

Hippolyta is right; what an unreasonable passion! This kind of feeling is no respecter of persons, of tastes, of preferences. Anyone who says, "I love X because we have so much to talk about together" or "because she is good, or because she loves me, or because I admire her" is lying or doesn't love. There is a kind of love-feeling, one of *two* basic kinds (the other is dependence-love) which is utterly impersonal—it seizes one, + whom it fixes on may be a perfectly grotesque object. If this love is hopeless, there is no use reviling oneself—suffer it, let consciousness of its manifest grotesqueness help it to pass.

By grotesque I don't mean immoral. This feeling is amoral, as well as impersonal. Burning cheeks; the ground slips from under your feet.*

*Remember the sight of E.L. that spring day out the window of the A10 English class (Miss Estrop)—how the desk top swerved and plummeted under my elbows. I had the same sensation—all so entirely involuntary + dissociated from feeling—as I helped David up the steps this evening at 6:30 after we returned from tea at the Carrs' [*the Marxist historian E. H. Carr and his wife, close friends of PR and SS*]. I wasn't thinking of much, + suddenly the step dropped from under me as it were + I fell full against the door.

•

To say, "*I* love" for this kind of feeling is impertinent. It is just "love," which happens to possess me, and direct me to X. For the other basic kind of love, dependence-love, it is proper to say "*I* love"; in fact, here the "I" is more important than the "love"

Additional note: In saying love is arbitrary I mean it is *experienced* as arbitrary. It is perfectly obvious, of course, that it is conditioned by suppressed longings, images, etc., etc.

For each person there is a very limited range of types of people he [*this "he" is crossed out in the notebook but no other pronoun put in its place*]—could fall in love with in this way.

For instance, I could never fall in love with someone who was—what?

•

*[Undated list of social events—presumably written in very early December but covering the last days of November 1956.]*

[*No date*]
dinner-party here: Carrs, [Marxist émigré philosopher Herbert] Marcuse, [Louis] Hartz, us

Saturday Nov. [*no other dating*]
dinner at the Carrs' (Brandeis): Carrs, Owen Lattimore, John Carter Vincent, me

Saturday, Nov. 24—
4:00–6:00 tea at the Carrs' (Brandeis) to take some stuff in for them: Carrs, we three

Nov. 26
dinner here: us, Carrs, walked them back to Ambassadors

Nov. 29
9:00–1:00 coffee; eye doctor's app't—Morgan Memorial; coffee

Dec. 1
tea at the Carrs' (Ambassador): us 3; brought chair

Evening: *The Cabinet of Dr. Caligari* (192[0]) Conrad Veidt, Werner Krauss, *The Last Laugh* (1925). Director: F. Murnau

12/13/56

Today, for the first time, the coherence theory of truth made sense to me. The truth of a statement judged by its coherence with the other statements we are obliged to make.

Correspondence can be subsumed here—as one of (the main?) the criteria which oblige us to include a statement in the system of statements.

Kant exemplifies the coherence theory of truth in his method of critical regress.

•

Thesis topic: "The Normative and the Descriptive" (?)

•

Lucretius' analysis of religion is like Freud's. Religion doesn't appease anxiety but awakes anxiety.

For both, the entire analysis is in terms of the category of anxiety.

Ethic of emotional non-commitment, disengagement seems to go along with this attitude toward religion. Again, Lucretius and Freud.

Also *this* ambivalence: the Promethean strain (exalt human, overthrow spurious divine; human autonomy + self-reliance) coupled with the ethics of prudence, the calculation of emotional expenditure.

12/15/56

Philip's thirty-fourth birthday.

Had some good ideas in Section 8A this morning on "Job."
Just as [William] James distinguished between a tender-
minded and a tough-minded way of doing philosophy, so one
can distinguish—a lot more usefully, I think, between a ten-
der- and a tough-minded way of doing religion. Tender-
minded religion assumes that the claims of *religion* + ethics
coincide; it is abhorrent, inconceivable for them to do otherwise. Tough-minded religion allows for this disjunction, even
opposition, between religions + ethical claims. The N[ew]
T[estament] is typically tender-minded; the O[ld] T[esta-
ment] (cf. the story of Abraham as interpreted by S[øren]
K[ierkegaard]; the Book of Job) is tough-minded.

The religious claim is from god to man; the ethical claim is
what governs the relation of men to each other.

•

Lunch with Joyce + Ted Carr

•

Tonight David—on the dressing table in the bathroom,
being prepared for bed by Rose—said: "How do people have
two husbands? When one dies?" I answered: "That's right.
If one dies, you can marry again if you want." To which he
answered: "Well then, when Daddy dies I'll marry you." I
was so startled + delighted that I could only reply: "That's
the nicest thing you ever said to me, David."

He seemed quite calm, but I was almost in tears—perverse super-sophisticated anti-Freudian incredulity, anxiety about how far Rosie has usurped David's affection for me, etc., etc., having led me to doubt he would *ever* say, spontaneously, anything classically filial + affectionate.

*[Undated, certainly mid-December 1956]*

From the *Journals* of S[øren] K[ierkegaard]:

> "There are many people who reach their conclu-
> sions about life like schoolboys: they cheat their
> master by copying the answer out of a book with-
> out having worked out the sum for themselves."

> ". . . the fantastic medium of abstraction."

·

No doubt about it, S.K. would have become a Catholic— according to the trajectory of the *Journals*. Those powerful final pages in which he analyzes Protestantism as a correc- tive, an antidote—but empty + unspiritual when established by itself, as in the Lutheran State Church of Denmark.

12/19/56

David knows the difference between a sarcophagus and an esophagus.

12/23/56

At the Gardner Museum [in Boston] (with David, Joyce Carr). "The pink flesh of Eden." Dewy bodies, barely nubile.

[American painter John Singer] Sargent's painting of Mrs. Gardner is a sort of shrine on the third floor. Long, thin picture; the hourglass figure of Mrs. G., heavy four-dimensional ropes of pearls, smudged mouth—as if the painter had drawn it very precisely, then passed the fleshy end of his palm across it while wet.

12/24/56

The Carrs for dinner tonight . . .

Philip is not going to read a paper after all—

David, very obliging and tender as he prepares for bed, whereupon this dialogue. "What if God never made the world?" I: "Then we wouldn't be. That would be too bad, wouldn't it?" He: "*Wouldn't* be? Not even Moses?" I: "How could anyone be, if there weren't a world to be in?" He: "But if there wasn't a world, where would God be?" I: "God exists before the world. He isn't a person or a thing." He: "Then if God isn't a *person*, why did he have to rest?" I: "Well, the Bible *speaks* of God as a person, because that's the only way we can imagine God. But he isn't really a person." He: "What is he? A cloud?" I: "He's not any *thing*. He's the principle behind the whole world, the ground of being, everywhere." He: "*Every*where? In this room?" I: "Well, why not? Sure." He: "Is God good?" I: "Oh, yes." He: "Is God the goodest thing there is?" I: "That's just right. Goodnight."

12/26/56

Interpretation:

Always the presumption of *meaning*. One criterion of interpretation (cf. Avril criticizing Cornford on the "Sophists") is
that it doesn't allow *enough* meaning (sense) to the text.


12/27–29/56 New York

left Dec. 27 with David—D wearing Oxford grey pants. Sub-
way to [Boston's] South Station. 8:00 train . . . In N.Y. 12:15.
Took a cab to the Gov. Clinton [Hotel]. Checked in, washed,
took cab via Empire State Bldg. to Golden Horn restaurant.
Ate shish kebab. Cab to Metropolitan Museum. 3:00–5:00 the
Egyptian exhibits and the Etruscan Warrior. Rosie arrived.
Bus back to hotel. Washed and changed. Left at 6:10—David
clinging to TV, Rosie about to whisk him across the street to
Penn Station + out to Flushing [*where Rose McNulty's fam-
ily lived*] for the night. Took cab to Hotel Taft. Herbert &
Inge [Marcuse] there, Peter + Frances arrived a few
moments later. Walked to Parisienne restaurant. Rushed,
lobster dinner. Walked back to Winter Garden [Theater].
*Troilus and Cressida.* Afterwards, with Tommy + school
chum added, went across the street to the Taft bar for beer.
Tommy + chum left, then Peter + Frances to drive back to
Waterbury [Connecticut]. Walked with Inge + Herbert to
subway at Columbus Circle. Goodnight. Back to hotel.
Asleep by 2:00.

Awakened at 10:00 by knocking at door: David + nurse [*Rose
McNulty*]. Dressed. David at TV again. At the first commercial, turned the set off. Downstairs + into a cab to the

Museum of Natural History. Two hours there. Bought David a Tyrannosaurus. Left at 1:00. Took bus down Central Park West. Got off at 51st St. And ate at Anchovy House. David had a bacon sandwich. Called Philip at 2:15. Walked D + nurse to subway (them to go back to Gov. Clinton, then to Penn Station for train to Flushing). Across the street, the Winter Garden. Bought matinee ticket. *Troilus and Cressida.* Back to hotel by 5:45. Read *N.Y. Times*, washed, changed. Called Peter Haidu. Left at 7:15. I walked six blocks, then took bus to 45th St. Bought ticket for *Cranks.* Looked about for restaurant. Went into Adano on W. 48th. At 8:30 left and walked over to Bijou [Theater]. *Cranks.* Funny. Out at 11:45. Cab to E. 73rd St., apt. of Alfred Clayburgh. Party given by [the American poet] Richard Eberhart. At the party: Eberhart + wife with the pig's snout, Oscar Williams, two Indians in costume, Tambinetta + wife, young poet named Gregory Corso wearing 18th c. specs, Jose Garcia Villa, Elaine Snyder (from U. Conn [*University of Connecticut, where SS had been a lecturer for one year, commuting from Boston*]; now working for the New American Library), fat poet named Oswald de Winter, Arabel Porter (of *New World Writing*) + husband John, Elizabeth Kezley (?) from Seattle, Jean Garrigue, Allen Ginsberg (poet).

Walked back to hotel. Sat in lobby with Corso for a half hour. Went up to the room at 5:30. Read *Times*, undressed, went to sleep.

Was awakened at 6:30. Dressed. Rosie + David arrived at 6:50. Left room + checked out of hotel by 7. Cab to Grand Central. (Roof ticket.) On 7:30 train to Boston.

12/31/56

1. Nothing is uninterpreted.
2. To interpret is to determine, restrict; or to exfoli-
   ate, read meaning into.
3. Interpretation is the medium by which we justify
   context.
4. To interpret a word is different from defining
   it; it means to specify a range of contexts
   (*not* equivalents).

.

kisses like bullets, soap-flavored kisses, kisses from lips that
feel like wet calf's-brains.

Let go
Let go
Let
Really go.

.

[Harvard psychologist] Jerry Bruner: How does X judge that
Y is his friend (likes him)? Women tend to judge on the basis
of *giving* behavior—if Y has given X presents, etc., X judges
that Y likes her. Men tend to be suspicious of giving-behavior
(thought to be homosexual?), judge on the evidence of agreement. X judges that Y likes him if he agrees with him.

.

One sense of "interpretation": making allowances for.

As a child, I was a feverish little Deist

# 1957

*[Dated only 1957]*

What *do* I believe?

    In the private life
    In holding up culture
    In music, Shakespeare, old buildings

What do I enjoy?

    Music
    Being in love
    Children
    Sleeping
    Meat

My faults

    Never on time
    Lying, talking too much
    Laziness
    No volition for refusal

•

Re-read: [Gertrude Stein's] "Melanctha," [Kafka's] *The Castle*


1/1/57

Ideas for stories—

Famous Jewish émigré—scholar / theologian, now "gentleman" from Harvard. Receives a prize from Germany. Goes to negotiate for Harvard for library of old Jew—a businessman [who] had a famous autograph collection; had made small benefaction to Kaiser Wilhelm Museum just before the war. When 1939 came Nazis put collection in cellars + seals on the door, but the man was allowed to remain in the house. In 1944 the English + American bombers came, + destroyed most of the houses in the area, but this house remains standing

Frame story

Told in abstract style—with as little factuality as possible.

Model: Kafka


1/3/57

I can remember what it was like not to be married—what I did—, but I can't feel like I was then. The sense of not being free has never left me these six years. The dream of a few weeks ago: a horse came up behind me as I was going down a short flight of stairs—into a swimming pool, it seemed—and placed its two front legs on me, one over each shoulder. I screamed and tried to free myself from the weight, then awoke. An objective correlative for my darker moods.

Goethe declared that only insufficient knowledge is creative.

## 1/5/57

Evening's conversation (7:00 to 1:00 a.m.) with Zeno Vendler, S.J. The Catholic Church is the only viable religious institution in the Western world. He's not unwilling to acknowledge the stupids and the fascists (Spellman, Mindzenty, etc.) or that it's foolish for the Church to have Descartes' *Discours* or [Victor Hugo's] *Les Misérables* on the Index. Of course, he's an intellectual, the house egg-head among his fellow Jesuits (how revealing: he said that his colleagues want him to appear on the $64,000 quiz show; Aunt Fanny said the same to P). Also the sense he gave of the Church's being above the Cold War: They could work in America, with [Władysław] Gomułka [*the Communist leader of Poland at the time*], with Franco, with [Imre] Nagy [*the leader of the Hungarian uprising of the previous year*] if he hadn't "gone too far."

There are 33,000 Jesuits in the world—8,000 in America, the largest number, 7,000 in Spain. Big fight within the order is between the Americans + the Spaniards.

After Zeno left, P + I sat for an hour's P.M. [postmortem]. What could Judaism do to compete with this? I raised the old objection: a religious vocation within Catholicism is still impossible for me, because the Church is so patriarchal—but the Jews are even worse in that respect. Where in all Jewish history is there a St. Teresa, an Edith Stein, not to speak of Mother Cabrini.

P said: Well, then, Judaism must be reformed. How would you go about it? I said: The first step would be the creation of an order—the Society of Maimonides, what you will. The Jews must remake a place for the religious vocation apart from the rabbinate—as the rabbinate has degenerated completely on the present congregational system, with an ignorant vulgar laity hiring a performer.

Would this order be coeducational? Yes. We would want to break the stranglehold of men. Would they take vows? There's the problem. Probably the Anglican system would be better—vows for a stated length of time, three years, six years, to be renewed. Poverty, chastity, + obedience? Judaism is a radically unascetic religion, + there's no precedent for chastity. But it doesn't make sense spiritually to compel people to remain unmarried without specifying that they remain chaste. Otherwise you encourage promiscuity, + the Order is no more spiritual than West Point. But what of chastity as a life-long vow? Is there any alternative to the sexually segregated paramilitary organization of the Church? P suggested a plan which reminded me of the Bruderhof.

1/6/57

Getting a cold. Mother called today. Dull academic evening, here: Jerry Bruner, the Rostows.

•

Read Gide's "Theseus" again.

On marriage: That's all there is. There isn't any more. The quarrels + the tenderness, endlessly reduplicated. Only the quarrels have a greater density, diluting the capacity for tenderness.

The leakage of talk. My mind is dribbling out through my mouth.

My will is more flabby than it's ever been before. Let this be the dip before the upswing.

•

Titles for stories: "Metropolitan Days," "Private Behavior" —these would be good for unified collections of stories. "The Promotion," "Diary of a Dun"

•

Two people handcuffed together next to a dungheap shouldn't quarrel. It just makes the dungheap a few inches higher, + they have to live with it stinking beneath their noses.

Quarrels are appropriate to friendships. But people who have to live together oughtn't quarrel.

P says he's sorry we quarreled because I had a migraine afterwards. A sad reason. A good reason is that it's senseless to quarrel.

•

Notes on Marriage

To be presented to my great grandchildren, on my golden wedding anniversary? "Great Grandma, *you* had *feelings*?" "Yeh. It was a disease I acquired in my adolescence. But I got over it."

•

P.: "You don't know what it's like . . . getting ready to write. One sits down, pen in hand, paper on a board. Get ready, on your mark, get set, stand up: ok, here goes. Ready, aim, write . . . The idea of writing has driven every idea out of my head."

. . . "It's so painful to be always at the starting-point . . ."

"I hate to be so self-conscious."

•

From now on I'm going to write every bloody thing that comes into my head.

A kind of foolish pride which comes from dieting on high culture for too long.

I have diarrhea of the mouth and constipation of the type-writer.

I don't care if it's lousy. The only way to learn how to write is to write. The excuse that what one is contemplating isn't good enough

•

The most precious thing is vitality—not in any sinister [D. H.] Lawrentian sense, but just the will + energy + appetite to do what one wants to do + not to be "sunk" by disappointments. Aristotle is right: happiness is not to be aimed at; it is a by-product of activity aimed at—

•

Ideas for stories

1. Story in the manner of Kafka: Academic awaiting a promotion. The over-interpretation of behavior. The Chairman of the Dept. The President. Letters of recommendation. Offprints. Not sure where power resides. Rumors. "Each time I came down the long corridor, he'd duck into the men's room. There was no mistaking that. Nature couldn't call with such stunning regularity."

2. A couple in a waiting room. The curious inter-section of private + public behavior.

•

1/14/57

Yesterday David announced, as he was being prepared for bed, "You know what I see when I shut my eyes? Whenever I shut my eyes I see Jesus on the cross." It's time for Homer, I think. The best way to divert these morbid individualized religious fancies is to overwhelm them by the impersonal Homeric bloodbath. Paganize his tender spirit . . .

*[Dated only January 1957, SS's long evocation of her child-hood, written in a notational, almost stream-of-consciousness manner is, apart from a few very autobiographical short sto-ries like "Project for a Trip to China," and a handful of inter-views, the closest she came to straightforward autobiographical writing. SS intermittently considered writing not so much a memoir as an account of her friendships with a few people—Herbert Marcuse and Joseph Brodsky being the names she mentioned most frequently. But in the end, she preferred to write fiction and, despite frequently vowing to do so, could never entirely succeed in curtailing her writing of essays. There are two versions. In the first, SS seems to have set down whatever she remembered, but in no particular order. The entries that are crossed out in that version form the bone struc-ture of a second, more ordered version. I have included long excerpts from the first version, while reproducing the second in its entirety.]*

NOTES OF A CHILDHOOD

*[First Version]*

Gammon + spinach. Anthony Rowley.

On the train to Florida: "Mother, how do you spell pneumonia?"

Sitting on Gramp's bed Sunday morning.

The dream of the Grove St. School being on fire.

The I.G.C. Miss Ruth Berken. Judy Weizman. Peter Kessner. Walt Fleigenheimer. Marcia Millard.

All the lies I told.

Daddy telling me to eat the parsley, it's good, in the Fun Club.

The big white blister on my finger when some paper caught fire from the Bunsen burner (I had my chemistry equipment in the small roll-top desk).

Thelma de Lara. The picture of Jesus in the basement. "That's a picture of God."

(8) Mother telling me she was going to marry Nat.

Sharing a room with Mother the first two years in Tucson. (Nat recommended it.)

Reading Ida Tarbell on the Duponts.

Finding a Kosher restaurant for Grandma.

The Normandy Isle School. Ida + Leo Huberman.

Chemistry sets.

Peter Haidu putting his hand on my thigh under the water (age fourteen).

Coming home to a barbecue dinner.

Crying in the movie *For Whom the Bell Tolls*—with Mother, in a big Manhattan theatre.

Poison ivy. Dr. Stumpf.

The ebony swinging doors (Chinese) that gave on to the living room in the house in Great Neck.

The table Christmas tree in Florida: silver with blue lights.

Wanting a sapphire.

Capturing grasshoppers to put on the keys of a toy piano.

Scraping my right knee at the Grove St. School.
Sitting down the teaching [*sic*], lifting my right leg
up to clean it off, trying to wipe the black mole off.

Writing a paper for Mr. Shepro on the four
California robber barons (Huntington Hartford,
Mark Hopkins +). [*Mr. Shepro was SS's favorite
teacher at North Hollywood High School. He was
blacklisted a few years after she graduated.*]

Daddy's pigskin wallet.

David Solomon, the grocer's son.

Admitting that I stole the dime when I didn't
(Great Neck School).

Reading Warden [Lewis] Lawes' *Twenty Thousand
Years in Sing Sing*, [Charles Wood's] *Heavenly
Discourse*, and *Les Misérables* (Forest Hills).

Our phone: Boulevard 8-8937.

The boarded-up house off Queens Blvd.
(Forest Hills).

Jealousy toward Margie Rocklin for having been
born in China + having an Amah. Embarrassed at
Uncle Aaron seeing my bottom while I was taking
a sun bath, but afraid to say so. (Great Neck).

Nellie [*housekeeper during SS's early childhood*].
Her room. The small radio on top of the dresser,
on the right as you walked into the room.

Arvell Lidikay being nice to me at Catalina Jr. High;
I didn't know how to be nice back.

Coconut trees in our back yard in Florida.

Mother was with Unk at a ball game on Dec. 7
[1941] when Uncle Aaron called to tell the news.

~~Using an electric plate at the El Conquistador.~~

~~The woman in back whose husband had TB.~~

Finding, building a fort.

Sidney Lidz ("Mr. Lidz") and his crooked face.

Uncle Ben in a brown suit.

The basement of the insane asylum in Verona
[New Jersey]. Smell of urine.

Sleeping with a Bible under my horse-hair pillow.
Taking it along when Mother took me for a weekend visit to Yonkers, Mt. Vernon? Ferry ride.

Mt. Arrowhead. Two weeks Nat commuted there.
The movie about the Brontë sisters.

The de Tolnay book on the Sistine Chapel in the
public library. Judith [*SS's younger sister*] carsick.

Camp Arrowhead. Full of terrors. Started biting
my nails.

Seeing Charlene's appendicitis scar at the Himmel
Pool.

Getting burns on my feet—in a walk on the out-
skirts of the El Conquistador property.

Buying a used copy of [Freud's] *Civilization and Its
Discontents* at Pickwick's [bookstore in Los Angeles].

Miss Berken lived in Woodside with her mother.

Sitting on the Sheffield milk box with Unk.
Telling him about "The Rusted Knight"
(story on "Let's Pretend").

Seeing Florence + Uncle Sonny kiss.

The egg-timer on the wall in the kitchen (Verona).

Seeing *Penny Serenade* [at the] Forest Hills Theatre
with Rosie.

Tucson: At night, from my upper bunk, testing
Judith on the capitals of all the States in the U.S.

The Chandler St. "Red Car" [Los Angeles].

Martha and Bill Hirsch. Suzie. When Martha came
for an afternoon to the house (Tucson) M + she sat
on the patio. Martha smoked Viceroys + I saved
the filter of one she'd smoked.

. . .

A nurse named Violet when Rosie was gone.

Seeing midgets at the [1939 New York] World's Fair.

Once, at a party at Miss Berken's apartment,
I spilled something on a chair.

. . .

Trying to bite my toenails when my fingernails
ran out.

Playing miniature golf at the Sunshine School—
with Frances Francis and the N.Y. boy, the two
eighth graders.

Learning that the Cord Meyer Apts. next door were
"restricted."

. . .

Turnips for lunch at the Sunshine School. Beans.
Expelling gas.

Seeing *Wuthering Heights* with Charlene Paul.

. . .

Aunt "Dan." The deep wide scar on her leg.

Seeing *Blossoms in the Dust* (Greer Garson)
with Mother.

. . .

Aunt "Dan's" birthday, April 1.

Daddy died Oct. 19, 1938.

. . .

Going to church with Rosie.

The lady next door in Great Neck who said her
father died. How? His heart stopped. Oh.

. . .

Tucson: Tumbleweed.

Discovering Thomas Mann in Clifton Fadiman's
*Reading I've Liked.*

. . .

The big white headboard on M.'s double bed.
(Forest Hills).

The train ride down to Florida.

Grandma Rosenblatt in Florida.

. . .

Rosie's family. The day they took me fishing.
"I want fish." It was an eel.

. . .

Milk with vanilla flavor in it, + peanut butter
crackers. (Forest Hills).

Reading Compton's encyclopedia.

Stopping my bike, coming home from school,
every day to look through the leaves of a big tree
to the sky.

Riding my bike through the University of Arizona.
"Bear Down" in big white letters on the roof of
the gym.

. . .

Hearing a concert by Soulima Stravinsky at the
Wilshire Ebell [in Los Angeles].

Sophia taught volleyball at one period.

The boy Peter, without feet + proper hands.

Waiting to live as Richard Halliburton [American
traveler and adventurer] did.

. . .

The "orgy" with E and F (summer '50).

L. She joined the Marines.

Putting my hand in dog shit under the bushes.
(summer in L.I.)

. . .

Sophia's house. Built by Gregory Ain.

. . .

Reading about Dr. Norman Bethune [*Canadian doctor who served with Mao Tse-tung's army*] in the back of *True Comics*. (Forest Hills).

Seeing Peter through the door of the Arcade Room with his head in his hands. (North Hollywood High School).

The two dwarf girls. (North Hollywood High School).

. . .

G. Spending the night with her.

. . .

Dreams of being "David."

Elaine Levi. Elaine playing the flute. Lending her *Martin Eden*.

Evenings on the Roof, the Wilshire Ebell Theatre.

Being caught at the Pickwick Bookstore for stealing *Doctor Faustus*.

The North Hollywood High School pennant on the wall of my room.

. . .

Forest Hills: Buying a book on China (vases, crafts, etc.).

Tucson: Running the hand mimeograph.
[*SS produced her own "newspaper" while the family was in Arizona.*]

Having my tonsils out. The nurse sat on my leg.

Petunias up the walk on both sides. (Verona).

Sleeping with Rosie. Hearing the train at night. (Verona).

The measles. 106. Riding in a car.

Walks with Peter in the hills near Coldwater Canyon.

Sheldon Kaufman. Too ugly to look at. Long white fingers.

The Hollywood Bowl.

Roommate at Cal: Alvajean Sinzik.

Audrey Asher, her smile.

Forest Hills: At the Station, telling Gramp he was the only one I'd miss.

. . .

Betting 25 cents on the World Series with Gramp. I for the Yanks, he for the "Bums"? [*Brooklyn Dodgers*].

Dreaming I could fly.

Reading Perry Mason novels. (Tucson).

[My] First Beethoven quartet: Op. 127.

Mr. Shepro. Eating in the teachers' cafeteria.

Sobbing on Mother's bony bosom before going to bed. Wanting to be better.

Mother slapped me on the face. (Forest Hills).

Dr. Berman, the dentist in N.Y. Wait's Topical Paste.

Eating at the House of Chan.

[Ravel's] *Alborada del Grazioso*. First [Hollywood] Bowl Concert.

Eating at Chasen's.

Learning to drive. The Dodge.

Riding on the subway. (N.Y. to Dr. Spain's).

Gramp said, "Eye-talian."

Peter + I translating *Walpurgisnacht* together.

. . .

Daddy-long-legs in the tent Gramp put up for me in the back yard. (Verona).

"Do you know the difference between the trachea and the esophagus?" (Verona).

The bonfire in front of the high school. (Verona).

. . .

Palm Springs. Deciding about God.

Irene Lyons. Buying cherries after we got off the "F" train. (I had come along with her when she went to meet her father.)

Daddy teaching me to whistle in the breakfast nook!

. . .

The "Camera Obscura" (in Santa Monica).

Playing gin rummy with Gramp.

Collecting travel info from Chambers of Commerce all over the U.S. The Drachman Travel Bureau.

"Land of Hope + Glory" at graduation.

Black-out curtains.

. . .

Eudice Shapiro and the American Art Quartet.

Going to Grauman's Chinese Theatre.

. . .

Judith's accident.

Mother wearing her hair piled up on top of her head. (Forest Hills).

Seeing *Medea*.

Daddy singing "She'll be comin' 'round the mountain when she comes."

. . .

Mom telling me Daddy is dead. In the living room.

. . .

Driving with Nat from Chicago to New York nonstop—Mother + Judith took a plane.

Arriving at Essex House [hotel in Manhattan].

The Flamingo Club. Drag show.

The Tropical Village in Santa Monica.

First kiss. Somebody from a Roof concert.

. . .

Listening on the floor to WQXR Hadyn quartet with Peter.

Seeing *The Cherry Orchard* (Charles Laughton) with Henia. (1949).

A performance of [Ben Jonson's] *Volpone* at the Actor's Lab with Mother.

. . .

Mother reading Leonard Lyons, *Redbook*, *Cosmopolitan.*

Pretending to take a shower at the end of gym period. (North Hollywood High School).

. . .

Coming to visit Mother in the hospital after Judith was born (with Rosie).

Florida: Dreaming that the Lone Ranger would come + carry me away on his horse, I wearing sandals.

. . .

Gounod's *Romeo and Juliet*. With Rosie.

Tucson: *The Phantom of the Opera* with Boris Karloff [*sic*]—while Mother was with Nat.

. . .

Ushering. In the balcony, hearing Rubinstein.

Giving Mother the campaign book by Henry Wallace.

The Sunday Mother came up to camp + I wouldn't swim for her.

Walking under the stars.

. . .

Hearing John Howard Lawson [blacklisted scriptwriter] speak. Has a limp.

Grandma Lena feeding me mashed potatoes. "One for Mommy, one for Judy . . ."

Wanting to grow up.

. . .

Weeping when Roosevelt died.

Listening to world premiere (radio) of Shostakovich's Seventh [Symphony].

. . .

Giving blood for Israel. The ache in my arm.

Dolores, chain of drive-ins; male car hops.

Uncle Aaron's wedding. The Essex House. The orchestra played "I Dream of Jeannie with the Light Brown Hair."

Bragging about Nat. [*Nathan Sontag was a highly decorated pilot, first with the British Royal Air Force, and then, after the United States entered World War II, with the American Army Air Force.*]

. . .

Copying the poems of Gerard Manley Hopkins.

. . .

Starting to collect stamps.

Having my own room. Choosing the colors.

. . .

Elaine said that the pretty gym teacher was a
lesbian.

When there was incinerator trouble in Grandma
Sontag's apt. bldg. (The Roosevelt), I panicked.

Fearing to fly.

. . .

Taking the Red Car downtown at 1:00 on Friday
afternoons to go to the Symphony.

. . .

Reading in *PM* [leftist New York newspaper] about
Bataan and Corregidor.

. . .

Going to a synagogue once in Tucson, hearing the
Rabbi ask everyone to cash in the War Bonds to contribute to synagogue fund drive.

. . .

The Valley Friends of Chamber Music. Franck's
Sonata in A Major. (Deborah Greene playing piano;
[her] husband the violin).

*The Magic Mountain.*

. . .

Losing my penknife + praying to find it. (Verona).

Uncle Sonny taking me far out in the water.
[*SS had a slight water phobia that she sometimes
attributed to this incident.*]

. . .

Daddy showing me how he folded his handkerchief.
(In their bedroom. Daddy dressing.) Telling
M[other] I would rather not be Jewish as she was
getting into the shower.

. . .

Rosie saving me wishbones of the first chicken +
the first turkey she cooked. Making a pot-holder
for Rosie.

. . .

Keeping Daddy's ring in a box.

Listening to Orson Welles' *Macbeth* (Mercury
Players).

Refusing to sun-bathe naked.

. . .

Going to a concert at Occidental [College, Los
Angeles]—the Alma Trio—in the rain. With Peter.
Wearing Mother's fur jacket. Hitching a ride for
part of the way back with a truck driver.

Daddy buying me a cash-register.

. . .

Royce Hall [UC Berkeley]: "The world is a progres-
sively realized community of interpretation."

Meyerhoff's course; talking with a cigarette in
his mouth.

The day F. Matthiessen died.

*[Second Version]*

FOREST HILLS (9–10)

The James Madison Apts.

Cutting up *PM*.

Our ap't number: D41.

P.S. 3.

The World's Fair.

P.S. 144.

Judy Weitzman. "You little shrimp—I mean eel."
Her mother, from Boston, fat. Said tomahto.

Taking a bus to school. Catching it on 68th St.,
in back of the Thomas Jefferson Apts.

Dr. Will Cook Spain. Infections. Reading comic
books in his office.

Feeling sad when Mother sold the car to a "defense
worker."

Aunt Pauline took me to see *Fantasia* (NYC).

Friday dinner at Grandma Rosenblatt's. Chicken
soup + boiled chicken. The old-fashioned radio with
legs in the living room. (NYC).

My book on rationing.

Telling Alice Rochlin that Tchaikovsky was better
than Beethoven.

Contracts.

Judy slept on a cot.

Going to "Jersey" through the Holland Tunnel.

Seeing *Life with Father* with Mother. My second play (age eight).

68-37 Yellowstone Blvd. [Queens, New York].

Reading the books of Albert Payson Terhune.

Johnnie Waldron. He taught me to use chopsticks.

A Chinese restaurant, "Sonny's" on Queens Blvd.

Dreams of Daddy coming back, opening the ap't door.

Telling Dr. Taschman I wanted to be a doctor.

Going with Mother to the "knitting" place (a Mrs. Greenberg) on 79th Street + B'dway.

Waiting outside, feeding the pigeons.

The vaporizer. Tincture of benzoine in cotton.

Hearing Shostakovichs's Fifth Symphony on the radio.

Miss Slattery at P.S. 3.

Christmas tree decorated by other and Unk + Mother's party.

Passing the tennis courts.

Writing an essay "On Time," headed by the drawing of an hourglass. "What is time? . . ." etc.

Writing my book on Russia.

Getting the Mercury [Theatre] records of *Macbeth*.

I sat on the toilet seat singing while Rosie rubbed my hair dry.

Looking at the book in woodcuts by Lynd Ward (*Gods' Man*) + being frightened—esp. by the last page.

Being hit on the head with a rock. All the blood on my white blouse. Judy Weitzman was with me.

Working for CD.

Buying Mother [Carl Van Doren's] *The Secret History of the American Revolution* for a birthday present.

V-mail from Uncle Sonny.

Reading comic books in Dr. Spain's office.

Sabu.

Self-service elevator in the James Madison.

Hy Hodes, on the living room sofa.

Eating at the Ham 'n Eggery with Mother. She picked me up at school during the lunch hour.

Mr. Lidz gave me Fuzzy.

Listening to the Hit Parade (radio) every week with Rosie.

Making a speech for Dean Alfange (for mayor).

Esther could play the piano "like the Philharmonic." She wore a white fur jacket.

We didn't have a terraced apartment.

Going to the Planetarium.

Mother knitting cablestitch sweaters.

Having a tantrum—Mother and Unk were there—about not wanting to be a girl when I grew up. "I'll cut my breasts off."

Crying because I was deprived of a Lone Ranger program.

". . . a wealthy + titled Englishman."

Stella Dallas + her daughter Lolly + Lolly's husband Dick Grosvenor [film with Joan Crawford].

"Lorenzo Jones + his wife Bella who loves him."

In the IGC. "May I have your attention, please?"

The room in P.S. 144 was 333.

Thinking three was my lucky number.


TUCSON (10–13)

Using an electric plate at the El Conquistador.

The woman in back whose husband had TB.

"The Hole." Digging it, filling it, digging it again.

The Lims (Chinese family who ran a grocery store on Speedway).

"A" Mountain.

Sabino Canyon.

The ducks in the garage: Laurie + Billie. Four chicks, too.

Getting Lassie. In the garage the first night.

At Mansfield Jr. High: Mr. Farrell, Miss Kalil,
Jim Billingsley, Dick Matteson, the fat boy Jimmy
who tormented me.

No good at algebra.

Watching the rodeo.

Going for swims at the Himmel Pool. (Mother
didn't approve at first.)

Judy played with Nichie.

2409 Drachman St. Phone number 5231-W
(no exchange).

Paulette Goddard at the El Conquistador pool.

No. 4 Speedway Bus.

Michael Pister.

Josephine Peabody, *The Pied Piper*.

Gramp sent me a real bow + arrows.

The Drachman Chemistry Club.

David Rose. His house burned down so we let
him in.

Starting my journal. The first entry was on seeing a
dead rotting dog on Speedway, near the Lim's store.

Miss Kalil said she loved Gilbert + Sullivan.
Said she saw Katharine Hepburn.

Becky.

Nat in his uniform.

Mother's Sunday School.

The Squtt children: Marcie + Vera
(from Minot, N.D.).

Our play about Goebbels. *Truth.*

Nat stayed at the Arizona Inn.

Nogales. The Cave (restaurant).

Intending to name my dog Lad.

The dentist, Dr. Fee, in the Bank Bldg. on Congress
St. He found six fillings.

Not allowed to go alone to the Lyric Theatre.

Ilse Sternberg. Riding. Horse named Gringo.

K. D. Anderson, principal of Mansfield.

There were 6 Junior Highs in the city; the Negro
one was Dunbar.

Asking Mother to copy out [James Russell Lowell's]
"The Vision of Sir Launfal" for me.

Being editor of *The Sparkler* (Mansfield paper).

My own paper: *The Cactus Press.*

Eileen Davidson + Bertie: Bertie's big two front
teeth.

Going barefoot on the bus downtown.

Mr. Stanhouse. His daughter Enid.

Miss Kalil lending me Vernon Venable's book
on Marx.

Miss D'Amico, the Latin teacher.

Being on the radio.

Mrs. MacMurtie's 15-minute program every morning, "Sally Sears."

The Don Cossack chorus and Draper & Adler at the High School.

Being called a kike at Mansfield.

The lady who made dolls. Hetty.

Bob Stone (?) who wanted to marry Mother.

Bob + I building a fireplace with bricks + mud.

Fighting with a girl named Jody during gym period (softball).

Max Factor's feeble-minded son.

Tears came to my eyes as I related that Tarzan + Jane had a son.

The magic show.

Campbell Ave.

Fort Lowell Rd.

"Millie, Millie, we're glad to see you back."

The Bausch & Lomb prize.

Mr. + Mrs. Paul Hodges.

Bobby Prater, his smell.

The Keystone Liquor Co.

Pat Corelli.

Becky.

Watching the Rodeo from the tower of the El Conquistador.

Trick-or-Treat with Bob, Cy, + Nichie.

The policeman + his tall wife.

Reading *Arizona Highways* [magazine].

Being forbidden by M[other] to read [Lillian Smith's] *Strange Fruit*.

Steve Shuham.

Trying so hard to be funny in letters to Mother. ("Archibald Sidebottom").

Mr. Starkie at Sunshine School. The tour off Snob Hollow.

Weeding the clover out of the front lawn.

Some woman gave me a bottle of beer at the El Conquistador pool + I drank it.

Sleeping in a bunk bed with Judy.

Mr. Starkie telling me to read [Theodor Storm's] *Immensee*.

A slam book.

Bob + I trying to mix an ant killer in the lab.

Hymie + Lil Myerson + two daughters. The White House dep't store.

Dr. Vivien Tappan—her office in her house.

The State (movie theatre).

La Jolla (nightclub).

Pioneer Hotel.

Santa Rita Hotel.

Belt with a large buckle of soft silver.

Micky telling me dirty stories in the bathroom
(El Conquistador).

The car, a Buick, arriving on Drachman St. from
New York.

Carrot-haired Shirley Mandel next door.

Mrs. MacMurtrie.

The stomach-ache in the dining room of the
El Conquistador.

At Sunshine School: the girl in the 8th grade named
Frances Francis.

Charlene Paul. That agony.

Tunes in the juke-box by the pool (El Conquistador).

Collecting *Classic Comics* in the 8th grade.


1/15/57

Rules + duties for being 24 [*SS's birthday was January 16,
1933.*]

1. Have better posture.
2. Write Mother 3 times a week.
3. Eat less.
4. Write two hours a day minimally
5. Never complain publicly about Brandeis or money.
6. Teach David to read.

Last night Philip said, "I don't want to be self-conscious
any more. How I hate Hegel + all those who raise self-

consciousness as the highest attainment. I'm dying of self-consciousness!"

"Well, if you don't want me to tell you when you do those things, I won't."

•

Joyce speaking of Jane Degras: "She was as *mild* as any sucking dove."

This is it. That's all there is. There isn't any more.

If only I get the fellowship to Oxford! Then at least I'll know if I am anything outside the domestic stage, the feathered nest.

Am I myself alone?

I know I'm not myself with people, not even Philip—from that stems the constant sense of irritation, with him, with myself. But am I myself when alone? That seems unlikely, too.

Ongoing projects:

> "Notes on Marriage"
> "Notes on Interpretation"
> Essay: "On Self-Consciousness as an Ethical Ideal"

For interpretation:

> Interpretation as cultural transportation. When stories from the Scripture can no longer be believed, one interprets them.

The myth is "broken" in the prism of interpretation.

~~Find out a lot about:~~
~~To become erudite in:~~

~~1. Life and philosophy of Abelard~~
~~2. Marine biology, esp. jellyfish~~
~~3. Baron Bunsen~~
~~4. Philosophy of Spinoza~~
~~5. Book of Job~~

Read: *The Amberley Papers* [*The Letters and Diaries of Bertrand Russell's Parents*].

•

"He had two systems of interpretation to explain his failure." (Sartre)

*[Undated except as 1957, but most likely January or early February]*

A) begin to collect *prints* (real ones, not reproductions)
B) learn Greek

•

Otto von Simson, *The Gothic Cathedral*, Bollingen, 1956, $6.50

•

SLANG

"the soft sell" (vs. "the hard sell")
"get the lead out"
"an odd-ball"

*[Undated early 1957 lecture note]*

[Paul] Ziff: "understanding means *analysis* break-up for Hegel. 'Reason' is synthesis."

This is a dodge to avoid arguments of Hume. To see Hegel makes you appreciate Hume.

•

exhibition of German expressionists, Dada-ists, etc. (post—WWI)

Otto Dix (1891–)
George Grosz (1893–)
Max Beckmann (1884–1950)
Karl Schmidt-Rottluff (1884–)
Erich Heckel (1883–)
Max Pechstein (1881–)
Christian Rohlfs (1849–1938)
Ernst Barlach (1870–1938)

Käthe Kollwitz (1867–1945)

2 of foremost Dada-ists:
Kurt Schwitters (1887–1948)
Max Ernst (1891–)

•

article: Lucretius

•

. . . When is commendation disinterested? When techno-
logical

Relation of commending to *grading*.

. . . Thucydides, Nietzsche on how objectives of commendation lose their value . . .

•

. . . We want a *correspondence* theory of truth, but we may be
satisfied with a *coherence* theory of morality

•

One of the main strands in modern literature is diabolism—
that is, self-conscious inversion of moral values. This is *not*
nihilism, the *denial* of moral values, but their inversion:
still rule-bound, only now a "morality of evil" instead of
a "morality of good"

Examples:

1) de Sade—consider him as the inversion of Kant's
   kingdom of ends. All persons must be *forced* to treat
   each other as means. Like Kant, immoral behavior
   must be rational + consistent (i.e. universalizable).
   See materials on Sade's utopia in [Geoffrey] Gorer.

2) [Jean] Genet's *Deathwatch*—snowball = God, prison = world, grades of crime = moral grading, murder = grace, misfortune = felicity, blessedness. Two attitudes to crime: Green-Eyes—comes as act of grace, is given; [and] Georgie—must be willed.

[Parallel] to two Christian positions

*Nightwood*

•

It's wrong—does these writers an injustice, for they were *sincere*. To say they are / were inverted religious in disguise (cf., Catholic claim on Baudelaire). Their diabolism is genuine.

Nevertheless, their *work* is a kind of tortured testimony to the force of their values. No Saturnalia.

Without repression most of the year; no Black Mass without a regular one. But this is superficial.

*Parody*

This is the most forceful *denial* of these values—full of mockery—to use their form while inverting their content

Another example is Kafka (an atheist)

•

"Lit[erature] of Diab[olism]" is an important cultural instrument, however. Presents us with sharp antagonisms:

Kant or Sartre, Calvin or Genet. Makes us choose. Shocks us out of complacency.

•

"liberals" think if you have (a) you always get (b). Which is plainly not true.

## 1/19/57

re conversation last night at dinner with Alan Fink + Barbara Swan: Conventions vs. spontaneity. This is a dialectical choice, it depends on the assessment you make of your own times. If you judge that your own time is ridden with empty insincere formalities, you plump for spontaneity, for indecorous behavior even . . . Much of morality is the task of compensating for one's age. One assumes unfashionable virtues, in an indecorous time. In a time hollowed out by decorum, one must school oneself in spontaneity.

Met Joyce [Carr] at Widener [library at Harvard] at 3:45. Tea at Hayes-Bickford. Book-browsing in Tutin's. She bought Mrs. Humphry Ward for P. I walked her home, had a 5-minute sherry, + returned at 6:30.

Today, David is Ajax the Lesser + I am Ajax the Greater. Together we're "invincible," a new word he's learned. His last words as I kissed him goodnight + left the room tonight: "See you later, Ajax the Greater." Then, peals of laughter.

•

P and me, quarreling constantly when we talk to each other, which is rare. I have been cast in the role of husband-killer à la Dorothea Brooke Casaubon [*character in George Eliot's novel* Middlemarch].

Spent the evening until 2:00 a.m. reading "Mrs. Humph"

1/20/57

When David came into our room at 8:30, I asked him what he had been talking about with Rosie. "Oh," he said, "I asked her how the world exists."

I phoned Mother today so David could sing her "Home on the Range"

. . .

Emerson said: "A man is what he thinks about all day." Emerson the existentialist.

*[Undated apart from the year, but most likely January or February]*

STORY

Professor
Young bride

1. His boyhood—Jowettish [*nineteenth-century Oxford classicist Benjamin Jowett*] isolation of [an] American intellectual

2. They meet + marry > intellect vs. sex (the wife)
3. Departmental squabble: tastes power (the rival)
4. Florence—world of art, tourism—wife stiffens
5. [The husband] meets again male friend—has a claim on him—wife objects—the husband leaves her + job to nurse [the old friend]

2/14/57

In marriage, I have suffered a certain loss of personality— at first the loss was pleasant, easy; now it aches and stirs up my general disposition to be malcontented with a new fierceness.

2/15/57

Marvelous Gallic performance of [Richard Strauss's] *Ein Heldenleben* last night. The Wagnerian suet just pared away, and underneath music that is lean, crackling, military. [Charles] Munch took the orchestra through it more rapidly than I've ever heard, and managed to produce a Strauss that was sensuous but not voluptuous.

2/18/57

"My son, aged four, on first reading Homer"

Plump downy face
Slack with wonder.
I declaim.

The strange names are learned,
also the many results of Zeus' lust.

Horror follows horror.
Poor Patroclus.
See you later, Ajax the Greater!
My son is moved to tears upon
   learning that this Ajax, though
   strong, was a dope.
He is impassive before Hector,
   dead, abused, his bones
   bleached by fire.

Poor Hector. We are sorry for Troy. Poor Troy.
Nevertheless, my son would
   Rather be a Greek. They won.
This child accepts the mystery of
   Violence, as did the Greeks.
He is not repelled by the brevity
   Of their mourning, nor by the
   length of their delicious meals.

He moralizes, but briefly:
Helen was not worth it.

He understands why Achilles weeps,
   for his golden armor, his
   helmet, his shield, his greaves,
   captured by Hector, as much as
   for dear Patroclus slain . . .

*[Undated, most likely late February 1957]*

Fields to be interested in: 1) linguistics à la Bloomfield, 2) problem of historical knowledge; philosophy of history, 3) problem of philosophic disagreement, 4) stipulation, 5) body-mind problem, 6) the normative + the descriptive

•

[Paul] Tillich succeeded [Hans] Cornelius (Kant scholar— member of Marburg School) as Professor of Philosophy (Ordinarius) at Frankfurt. Taught Schelling, some Hegel. No Kant scholar. Had been Christian, + that was past.

Heidegger was successor to chair of Hermann Cohen at Frankfurt. Cohen dies in 1918.

[Nahum] Glatzer [*1903–1990, literary scholar and theologian, PR's colleague at Brandeis, family friend, and DR's god-father.*]

*[Undated, most likely late February or early March 1957]*

DON'T

1. Criticize publicly anyone at Harvard—
2. Allude to your age (boastfully, mock-respectfully, or otherwise)
3. Talk about money
4. Talk about Brandeis

DO

   1.  Shower every other night
   2.  Write Mother every other day

               •

. . . Kombu—Japanese seaweed (edible / is dried) comes from Northern Japan . . .

Part of the last mov[ement] of Beethoven's Ninth was inspired by the traditional music played by the Turkish military band called the Mahter, which also introduces cymbals + the drum into modern western music

               •

distinguish

   1.  death camps (Maidanek, Auschwitz, Oświęcim, Birkenau)
   2.  concentration camps (Buchenwald, Dachau, Sachsenhausen, Bergen-Belsen)

death camps were mostly in Poland + "processed" only Jews—opened in fall of 1942 + operated to fall of 1944, when Himmler closed them down

best source on death camps is Léon Poliakov's: *Bréviaire de la haine* (Paris, 1951)

*The Root Is Man*
—Dwight Macdonald
Alhambra: The Cunningham Press, 1953

3/19/57

If I thought about nothing else but logic, I think I could be good at it. But it demands such a "sacrifice of the intellect," paradoxical as that may seem

*[Undated draft of a letter to the principal of Somerville College, Oxford, most likely written in February 1957]*

Dear Dr. Vaughan:

1) Just got the Fellowship
2) Study philosophy in Oxford and carry on research project
3) Though I am going [as a Fulbright scholar, I hope to] read for the B. Phil . . .

*[In the margin]* Professor [Herbert] Hart has given me permission to use his name as a reference.

*[Undated note]*

Holland-America Line
Vandam
Rhinedam
Maasdam

Leaves [for England] from Hoboken
One-class ship
8 days
$260

3/27/57

Philip is an emotional totalitarian.

"The family" is his mystery.

An ejaculation of weeping.

•

1536—Henry VIII expropriated the English monasteries. This is a fact. But what does it mean? No one—no significant class or profession—lifted a voice in protest. It means that this institution, into which so many people had poured their heart + blood + mind, was *dead*. The world is cluttered with dead institutions. Who among us would lift a finger if our university were threatened, or the synagogues of America were expropriated by Gen. Eisenhower; who would [*crossed out: "lay down his life"*] defend the nation state if he were not conscripted?

The world is cluttered with dead institutions.

•

1805:  Napoleon's victory at Austerlitz
1809:  Tennyson born
1811:  Kleist's suicide
1813:  S.K. [Søren Kierkegaard] born
1814:  Napoleon defeated
1831:  Hegel died
1844:  Hopkins born
1850:  *In Memoriam* published
1855:  S.K. died

1856:   Freud born
1859:   *Origin of Species*
1861:   A. H. Clough died
1864:   [Dostoyevsky's] *Notes from Underground* published
1865:   Yeats born
1875:   Rilke born
1882:   James Joyce born
1885:   D. H. Lawrence born
1888:   Matthew Arnold died
1889:   Hopkins died
1892:   Tennyson died
1900:   Nietzsche died
1926:   Rilke died

*[Undated, most likely late March or early April 1957]*

For theory of language:

Limit of thought = language. Language is link between sensations + the world.

CONDILLAC

Read Condillac!

[Quote from H. L. A.] Hart: "He took me round the problem. It's like a labyrinth with a hundred doors; you pop in one, look about, then pop out again."

*[Undated but almost certainly summer 1957]*

read Virginia Woolf's cantankerous feminist *Three Guineas*
[also Cesare] Pavese, *The Moon + the Bonfires* (25 cents)
[and his] *Among Women [Only]*

8/29/57

Dreadful migraine last night; after taking my pills, I didn't
sleep; spent the night rushing from room to room—in bed
with P, who was exhausted from packing the car; rubbing my
lips against David's exquisite skin; chatting with Rosie in the
kitchen while she ironed and fried; making out checks and
aimlessly filing papers . . .

At 5:00 David cried out—I dashed to the room, + we hugged
+ kissed for an hour. He was a Mexican soldier (+ therefore
so was I); we changed history so that Mexico got to keep
Texas. "Daddy" was an American soldier.

He asked me this morning if I had ever been afraid. I told
him, yes, once—the time when the smoke from the incinerator filled the corridor of Grandma Sontag's apartment
building + I thought the building was on fire.

Philip and I never really had a chance to say goodbye properly—no long talk at any time during these last few days—
for it was only then that we stopped quarreling. I'm still
numb from that bitterness, + it trivializes everything to pretend all those bitter insults *weren't* exchanged.

There were tears and sexless tight embraces, and entreaties about health, and that was all. The parting was vague, because the separation still seems unreal.

I went in the house, took off the grey trench coat which I was wearing on top of my red pajamas, + went to bed. The emptiness of the house seemed so loud. I was cold, my teeth chattered, my head weighed 100 lbs—but I didn't really sleep, I drifted on the crest of sleep, holding off so I'd hear the Railway Express truck come to pick up the book box.

Rosie left 3 pieces of chicken + I ate one. Slept again. Brandeis Univ. Library called at 11:30 about unreturned books. Went out on the street around noon;—called R. Express to be mechanically reassured that a truck *would* come. Ate another piece of chicken. The truck came at 4:30. Fiddled with the mss. Mrs. Graham Greene called, in Boston for a day, looking at doll collections; wanted to know if any museums were open after 5:00 + what the good women's shops were. Filed + sorted some more papers.

Went out at 6:30 to the U.T. Popcorn. *An Affair to Remember* (Deborah Kerr, Cary Grant)—awful! And *A Kid for 2 Farthings* (Celia Johnson)—very good. I cried at the movie: the tender wise old Jewish tailor, the little boy who wanted a pet and was trusting + dark-haired. I cried at these!

Read a little in [Albert] Guerard's *Art for Art's Sake* (so cocksure + 20-ish) and was asleep by 12:00.

P called from London, Ontario at 1:30 to report a good trip— David cheerful, the dog pacified.

8/30/57

I was awakened at 8:00 by Special Delivery—the check for
the D.L.E.A. + traveling expenses 1/2 from the Center
($1400). Went back to sleep until 11:00. Sorted Freud papers,
filed things away (there's still more). Julius Moravcsik called
at 1:00, to say goodbye, + said he's gotten an apartment
[through] the English-Speaking Union, I must try that.
Dressed + went out at 1:00—first to the Harvard Bookstore
+ sold 4 books for $3.50, then to the bank to deposit the
$1400; then to the Coop + bought a refill for this notebook
(saw Marshall Shulman—he has a strong handshake); then
to [Prof. Morton] White's office (Widener U) at 2:30 to say,
"As Gertrude Stein said to William James, I don't feel much
like doing philosophy today." Made another app't for 11:00
Tuesday.

At Elsie's [sandwich shop in Cambridge]: a roast beef sandwich, open apple cake, water (65 cents). Returned home at
3:15. Continued to sort Freud materials, made notes, worked
on some rough passages in Ch. 2. [*SS is referring to* Freud:
The Mind of the Moralist, *the book she and PR worked on
together throughout most of the latter half of their marriage,
but which appeared under PR's sole authorship after their separation and subsequent divorce.*]

Moravcsik called at 5:00 to give me the address of the E-S
Union. Wrote them a letter, to a Mrs. K. L. Gee who helped
him. Wrote to St. Anne's [College, Oxford] too, telling them
the date of my arrival.

Went out at 7:30—walked to Central Sq. + gorged myself on
a passable pizza at Simeone's ($1.58). Saw the last hour of

*The Curse of Frankenstein* (Technicolor, sedate, English) at the Central Sq. theatre. Home by 10:30 (caught the bus on Mass. Ave. part of the way).

Stripped the beds in David's room.

P called at 11:00; said he'd called at 8:00, when they arrived at Chicago. Fine trip. Rosie at this minute out walking the dog. David sang "Wave the Flag for Old Chicago" for me—I talked to him twice. "I've been watching a detective story on television and, you know, they dropped a bomb!" (This was said twice). P thinks he'll drive, after all; it was so easy. He'll call tomorrow.

Drank a glass of cold milk.

I was going to take a shower + wash my hair, but felt too indolent. Read 54 pp. of *The Sun Also Rises* (dull) + fell asleep by 12:30.


8/31/57

Woke at 11:30. Cleared away a little more of the mess, transcribed some Freud notes, shelved stray books. Called Mandrake Book Store to see if I can get some wrapping paper from them, to send some more Freud scraps directly to St. Anne's. Worked some on the footnotes to Ch. 3. Went out at 3:30. Took the package to Mandrake to be wrapped, + will call for it Tuesday morning. Had a decent meal (spare-ribs and shrimps in soy sauce + black mushrooms) at Young Lee's for $2.79. The place was empty when I sat down, + only two other tables were occupied when I left . . .

Walked home around 4:45. Bought a *Times*. Read it in the dining room, while playing the *Carmina Burana*; drank a glass of milk; straightened some books in the shelf in the hallway; called Henri Weinhart to say goodbye (Me Being Polite), no answer. Called Mother at 6:30—an affectionate, unforced conversation. N is in Oregon, Judith is moving out tomorrow.

Went upstairs at 7:00. Washed out some underwear, + began to get ready to get ready [*sic*] to work on the paper for White. Slept an hour. Began around 9:00; Philip called at 10:00 (collect—his father's angry about the length of last night's call) + I spoke to David, too. P says he's arranging for a driver for Tuesday + they'll fly (!) on Friday. Read some more of the Hemingway. At 12:00, a shower—washed my hair. Browsed in White's book, trying to get myself in the mood to write his kind of paper. Asleep at 2:00—what a soporific.

9/1/57

Awoke promptly at 11:00. Sorted some more papers + books, the wastebaskets emptied, packed the rest of my suitcase. Played the *Nelsonmesse* + prepared myself 2 soft-boiled eggs + a glass of milk. Wrote David a letter, Henri Weinhart a note. To work on the White paper in earnest around 1:00. Quit around 2:00 to throw together a small can of tuna + a half jar of pickled mushrooms. Called the Gouverneur Clinton [Hotel in New York City] to make a reservation for Tuesday night. Worked 'till 4:30. Had a little packaged soup. Washed out my underwear and pajamas. Read some more Hemingway. Went out at 6:30. Walked a while on Brattle + side streets looking at roof moldings on middle 19th century frame houses. Went into the Brattle Theatre at 7:20 to see

*Three Forbidden Stories* (very mediocre—+ all cut to hell).
Walked home at 9:30. Two boys with grating N.Y. accents
half-heartedly trailed me from the movie, insisted when I
stepped into the street just in front of the house that their
car was parked on this street—would I like to go for a ride?
Heated up then ate the rest of the soup. Called Aron Gurwitsch on the phone to say goodbye; no answer.

I've been fighting against work all day—this is a stupid
paper, + I've no interest in it. In fact, I've no interest in philosophy at all at the moment. My mind's empty, I ache with
restlessness. I must have walked miles in this house in the
last three days. Before sleep (about 1:00) I finished *The Sun
Also Rises*; read 4 or 5 Hemingway stories + "The Fifth Col-
umn." What rot! as Lady A. would say.

9/2/57

Awoke at 10:00. (Why?) Fussed about upstairs, went downstairs and ate a soft-boiled egg, orange juice, + a dish of
apple sauce.

Spent an hour wrapping + cording up the thesis to mail off
tomorrow with the other stuff. (Just in case . . . I haven't time
to transcribe the few things I might need from it.) Now I
know why I tend to be sloppy, to heap things up when I'm not
using them. When I do try to be neat—to pick up after
myself—I become compulsive, obsessed; I waste hours at it.

Found some 3¢ stamps on an old envelope + spent another
half hour pasting them on my letters. Two trips to the mail-
box—because I discovered the edge of one stamp wasn't
glued, so I had to return to the house!

Made some notes on the Abrams book for Ch. 4 [and] on the footnoting style of [Lionel] Trilling's book on [Matthew] Arnold.

Ate some bean soup (with Riesling + lemon juice), opened a can of sardines. Called Gurwitsches—they were chilly. (Entertaining [the publisher] Kurt Wolff.) Tried to sleep for an hour.

Went for a walk at 4:00. Saw an hour of *The River's Edge* (Anthony Quinn) at the U.T. (Bearable—Technicolor). Home at 5:15.

Drowning in silence; neurotically tired, restless . . .

Worked an hour or so. Drank a glass of orange juice. Listened to a news broadcast. Brought the suitcases down to the living room. Called the railroad to see if there was a fast train at 2:00 as well as at 1:00. There is. Tried to call Rosa Goldstein to say goodbye—no answer. Poured a jigger of crème de menthe + went upstairs. At work in earnest at 8:00. Stopped at 10:30. Phone[d] P, who reports that things are horrendous and Balzacian in Chicago [at PR's parents] (Moneymoney)

In third gear—worked on until 6:00 a.m. + finished the idiotic thing. Set the alarm for 9:00.

9/3/57

*[I have chosen to reproduce SS's last day in Cambridge, and, in reality, the last day of her marriage, in the detail in which she set it down, but then omit her equally detailed account of her*

*train trip, arrival in New York, and what she did on the first*
*night she spent there.]*

at 9:00 my eyes were stinging but I was too tense to feel
exhausted, and getting up was no trouble. Straightened +
shoved away "last things," pasted Please Do Not Open stick-
ers on the files + card index boxes, retyped the last two pp. of
the paper, took a shower, dressed, + left the house at 10:30
laden with packages + envelopes of notes, clothing (to
Chicago), etc., to mail. Staggered as far as the Mandrake
Book Shop (no cab on Mass. Ave.), picked up the additional
packet they'd wrapped; left everything there + went across
the Square [*i.e., Harvard Square*] to get a cab, came back
with it to the bookshop, piled everything in + was driven 3
more blocks to the post office. (By now it was 11:10 and my
app't with White was for 11:00.) A helpful post office clerk
but it still took time . . . On my way to Widener I passed
White on Mass. Ave. going in the opposite direction; he'd
waited (but had things to do) + was now on some errands—
bookstore + bank. We agreed to meet in his office in 20 min.,
+ I spent the time at Elsie on a Rost Bif Special.

No one there when I knocked at the door of Widener U.
White came a few minutes later, bustling down the corridor,
let me in + we sat down for an hour of philosophical talk.
(Low-voiced, intense, occasionally playing at disagreement
but ultimately always agreeing) I asked him how much the
"therapeutic" aspect of [Ludwig] W[ittgenstein]'s doctrines
prevailed at Oxford, he said not much—only [John] Wisdom
at Cambridge took that sort of thing seriously. What about
[the philosopher J. L.] Austin's reported view that when
philosophers are really good + know what they're doing
there won't be philosophy any more, that philosophical problems are not to be *resolved* but *dissolved*—said I. Well, said

he (judicious-lee), he didn't think these views were the same. Austin thought *some* problems could be dissolved, but there was still work for philosophy to do. No one who heard his W[illiam] James lectures doubts that Austin was doing philosophy, + of a constructive sort. Etcetera, etcetera.

He asked me what I thought of [the judicial philosopher and former British Nuremberg deputy prosecutor H. L. A.] Hart's seminar—I was condescending, politely negative: the attitude I know he takes. Together "we" dissected the seminar. I said that the basic underlying analogy Hart drew (more— identity he posited) among the causal inquiries of the lawyer, the novelist, + the historian was at fault. They were all different—+ developed this along the lines of my paper: No distinction between *use* and justification, etc. *He* said (+ this was the only insightful remark of the hour) that what soured him on most of the work done at Oxford (Austin excepted, naturally) was that they seemed interested in a phenomenological description of unclarified discourse. Exactly, said I; and further, they hold that this is all philosophy can safely do—when you try to go further (à la the rational reconstructionists), you get "muddles," "puzzles," etc.—that have to be dissolved. White thought this was analogous to the fights among American economists between the "institutionalists" (e.g., Veblen) + those who were interested in constructing abstract models (or mathematical formulae) of economic behavior. Naturally, White thought that both were right and wrong, advocated a middle way.

The last part of the hour was spent chatting . . . [and] about where to stay in London + Oxford—he recommends the Linton Lodge in Oxford. He advised me to go to London to hear [the philosopher A. J.] Ayer and [Karl] Popper. He wrote a letter of introduction to Austin. (There was a bit of hostility expressed there re the "Miss Sontag.") A graceless exit, where first I went out the door + stood in front of the elevator, then he followed + got off on the second floor.

I went to the ground floor + out the back entrance on to Mass. Ave. + walked home. It was now 1:00. I shut the padlock on the kitchen closet, shut my suitcases, used the toilet, then called a Harvard cab which came in three minutes with a pleasant old man driving it. It was now 1:15. I directed him down Mass. Ave. (1) to stop in front of the Widener entrance so I could return a book ([John] Gay's *Plays*—Abbey edition, with the music); then (2) to the post office, where I mailed the rest of the packages, including one of old clothes to Chicago; then (3) to the Bradley offices on Brattle St., where I left a copy of the lease + the keys to the house with perspiring, disorganized Mr. Elliot; then (4) to Back Bay Station. It was just 2:00 when the cab got there, + the train was due in 5 minutes, + there were no porters anywhere in sight. The driver offered to carry my bags (this is against the rules) when I became slightly frantic—carried them into the station, where there were still no porters, + then down the stairs to the train which was just pulling in. For all this and the cab fare ($2.15) I gave him $4.00—he tipped his hat + wished me a good trip, the conductor put the bags aboard the train, + I was off.


9/5/57

*[The day of SS's departure by ship to England]*


*[After breakfast with her old friend from adolescence, Peter Haidu, by then an M.A. candidate at Columbia]*

I walked rapidly back to the hotel, went upstairs, took a shower, redressed, + closed my suitcases. It was now just 11:00 + I suddenly realized with a start that perhaps the 11:30 sailing time was seriously meant (unlike the sailing of the *Newfoundland* in Boston [*the ship SS and PR had taken to Europe in 1951—their one trip abroad together*]). I hauled the suitcases out to the elevator, demanded the bill in a hurry, wrote out a check, + got in a cab . . . [When I rushed up the gangplank there] was Jacob [Taubes, 1923–1987, sociologist of religion]—waiting for an hour he said. I was really touched—for who can afford *not* to be moved by the *gestures* of affection. I kissed him + boarded—he continued to wave until the boat was out of sight.

Once on board I had no patience—I was much too upset + distracted—to stand on the deck savoring the N.Y. skyline, etc., with the gapers + camera addicts, + I was relieved that the first sitting of lunch was immediately announced . . .

*[SS recorded her time aboard ship in great detail, but the entries are little more than notations of when she rose and went to bed, what she ate, etc. There are no entries concerning her arrival in Britain. This notebook takes up again with SS already in London.]*

9/17/57

Awoke at 9:00. Hiked to the toilet, then returned to bed to write last night's letter to P. Jane [Degras] called at 9:30— arranged to meet her for coffee at Chatham House [The Royal Institute of International Affairs London] around 11:00. Meant to get up for breakfast, but I *was* too comfortable. Wrote a letter to David about the Elgin Marbles . . .

. . . Walked a long way [with Jane Degras and a colleague of hers from Chatham House]—they insisted, searching for a bargain—to Santo Romano on Old Compton St. 4/6 [pounds/shillings] Table d'Hôte. I ordered rump steak. It came, diminutive + inedible. Dull conversation. After lunch left them + went to Foyles [bookshop] (very near); spent an hour in philosophy section. It's deteriorated hugely since 6 years ago. Bought nothing.

Starting to feel nauseous—my head pounding. [*SS suffered from severe migraines until she was in her mid-thirties.*] Walked left up Tottenham Court Road; saw a cinema featuring *La Romana* and *Riso amaro* and went in. Saw most of the first and all of the second. Bought a lousy vanilla ice between the films.

Feeling worse when I came out at 6:00. Caught a bus (#1) back to hotel, got undressed + went to bed. Slept until 9:30. Still in bed, I turned on the *Third Programme* + listened to the latter 2/3 of a new English translation of Gide's *play* of [his novel] *Les Caves du Vatican*. That was over by 10:45, + now my migraine was in full career. I should have taken something earlier, but somehow shrank from confirming it. One of the worst—within the next three hours I took 5 of the prescription + 3 codeine tablets, before getting any relief.

By 2 a.m. it had subsided, but I was up for the rest of the night as usual. Studied Italian for two hours, wrote letters to Minda Rae, Mother, + Rosie—+ a card to James Griffin—(I took his pen by mistake on Sunday). Re-read the *Muirhead Guide to London* + planned the places I'd take David. A lot of nervous energy expended in reading. At 6 a.m. began this entry, + will try to sleep now.

*[During the last week of September and the first week of October 1957, SS and Jane Degras went for a holiday in Italy. SS kept copious notes, but most simply record what she saw, what the trains were like, where the two women stayed, and what they ate. The only entry I have included is SS's description of Florence, which she was seeing for the first time.]*

Florence is so beautiful that it's madly unreal; the beauty of modern cities consists in a sense of their power, cruelty, impersonality, massiveness, + variety (as in New York or London) seen *against* the architectural vestiges of a beautiful past (as in Boston, a little; and much more so in London, Paris, Milan), but this is not the beauty one finds here. Florence is entirely beautiful, that is, entirely set in the past, a museum city, which has a present (souped-up Vespas, American films, tens of thousands of tourists—mainly American + German) but such is the grandeur, density + aesthetic homogeneity of the city that the modern elements—at least the Italian part—don't jar, don't spoil anything.

The city was not bombed during the war, but many old houses + buildings and all the old bridges with the exception of the most famous one, the Ponte Vecchio, were blown up by the Germans when they retreated in 1944. There is much new building going on, but the typical Florentine structure (red tile roof, three or four stories high, white or brown plaster walls, long windows with shutters that can be flung open) is being preserved + respected throughout.

The weather is perfect, warm enough to go about in a cotton dress or shirt sleeves at all times (the temperature doesn't drop in the evening, as in California) but never hot. I have a great window, seven feet long, in my room: I left the shutters entirely open all last night, + will do the same tonight . . .

. . . I was moved by the service this afternoon in the Santa Croce. There is really only one viable religion in the west. And Protestantism—how significant the name is; it has meaning as a protest, partly aesthetic + partly religious (so far as these can be separated) against the vulgar, overwhelming, oriental Catholicism. But without the Catholic Church it is meaningless + insipid . . .

*[Loose-leaf page, dated only Sept. 1957]*

unbearable to look at photographs of the face she had known in ecstasy and asleep.

*[Undated except as 1957—Oxford]*

Life is suicide, mediated.

This little cone of warmth, my body—its protections (nose, fingers) are chilled.

Speak of chilled fingers.

The private life, the private life.

Struggling to float my pieties, idealisms.

All st[atement]s *not* to be divided into true + false ones. This can be done, trivially. But then the meaning is mostly bleached out.

Being self-conscious. Treating one's self as an other. Supervising oneself.

What is the secret of suddenly beginning to write, finding a voice? Try whiskey. Also being warm.

10/15/57

*[SS kept copious notes of the classes she took at Oxford. This notebook contains the notes she took for a philosophy class taught by J. L. Austin. They are not reproduced here. Of significance in the personal sense, however, are some jottings SS made on the inside cover as she was gearing up for her move to Paris.]*

café crème—white coffee after dinner

café au lait—breakfast coffee

une fine (brandy)

un Pernod (as many Pernods as colas in the U.S.)

go to "Copar" Comité Parisienne, 15 rue Soufflot (street on which Pantheon is) get meal tickets to student restaurants, e.g., Foyer Israelite International Rest. [rue] M. Le Prince

get concert list—worthwhile from "Jeunesses Musicales de France" (student organization)—get cheap seats to concerts

inquire if there is a "tarif étudiant" at cinemas [and] galleries

•

*[Undated, but most likely late fall 1957]*

[Hieronymus] Bosch

Bosch drawing in a Dutch museum: a drawing of trees with two ears at the side, as if listening to the forest, + the forest floor strewn with eyes.

The picture spoke an unknown language, but it spoke it clearly + the emotion conveyed stirred one's depths

.

A. E. Housman b. March 26, 1859

11/2/57

Late yesterday afternoon I skidded on the bicycle + was thrown across the sidewalk. Last night I dreamed that I had a huge wound in my left side, blood fell out, I went about but I was dying.

11/4/57

Try whiskey. To find a voice. To speak.

Instead of talking.

.

Are the Jews played out? I am proud of being Jewish. Of *what?*

.

[Mucius] Scaevola—young Roman patrician who held his hand in the fire w/o flinching.

Tiki—the Polynesian and Maori god who is said to have created the first man. Hence, ancestor, progenitor; also designates a wood or stone idol made in the likeness of man

Charlotte Corday (1768–93)—girl who assassinated Marat (anti-Revolution)

Hathor—the Egyptian goddess of love + its pleasures. Often represented as having the head, horns, or ears of a cow

>     John Bull—GB
>     Uncle Sam—US
>     Jean Crapaud—Fr

Orc—imaginary mailed beast, dragon, ogre named after a sea-monster killed by Orlando, in Ariosto's *Orlando Furioso*

.

>     adventitious
>     penny-ante (job, situation)
>     fractious
>     captious

.

11/28/57

*[Loose-leaf page found among SS's papers]*

deracination

*Der Monat*—Berlin
Jews > Utilitariansim

Essence of Bohemianism is envy—must be a solid intel-
ligentsia to which it is peripheral—can only exist in certain communities—e.g., S.F., N.Y.—+, of course, the prep
schools or Bohemia—Chicago (College) + Black Mountain
[College], etc.

Morality informs experience, not experience informs morality

Philistine or
"substituting culture for inwardness"

creative error
extravagant mind—*connections*

morality [minus] self-interest = finding commitments,
loyalties—
either / or—indifference is support—
no pacifism—there is right hatred

cult of the holy prostitute:
Dostoyevsky, Lovelace

Love = death ("dark lady," femme fatale):
Wagner, D. H. Lawrence

Answer to [the "reverence for life" philosophy of Albert] Schweitzer—If all is valuable—even the ant—if the ant must not be killed, is as valuable as I, then, implicitly, I am as valueless as the ant—All people are not the same, worth the same—To allow an evil to happen is to assist the evil— There *is* righteous violence

Community—brotherhood—"How goodly"—middle-class way is unenjoyment, broken homes, systematic cheating—

Politics is the art of the possible—"protest vote" is?

Either are or aren't—aristocratic Judaism—either "one of us" or one of the Goyim [Gentiles / non-Jews]—perfect thy-self—there is an elect, an elite—


12/29/57 Paris

St. Germain des Prés. Not the same as Greenwich Village, exactly. For one thing, expatriates (Americans, Italians, English, South Americans, Germans) in Paris have a different role + self-feeling than provincials (e.g., kids from Chicago, the West Coast, the South) who come to New York. No rupture of national identification, and mal-identification. Same language. One can always go home. And, anyway, the majority of Villagers are New Yorkers—internal, even municipal expatriates.

The café routine. After work, or trying to write or paint, you come to a café looking for people you know. Preferably with someone, or at least with a definite rendez-vous . . . One should go to several cafés—average: four in an evening.

Also, in New York (Greenwich Village) there's a shared comedy of being Jewish. That's missing, too, from this bohemia. Not so Heimlich [homey]. In Greenwich Village, the Italians—the proletarian background against which the deracinated Jews + provincials stage their intellectual + sexual virtuosity—are picturesque but pretty harmless. Here, turbulent marauding Arabs.

*[Undated, late 1957: shortly after arriving in Paris, SS filled one notebook with thumbnail sketches of the people she was meeting, the world into which she was moving. The description of H. contains no acknowledgment of their relationship.]*

Mark Euher—from Detroit—thirty?—wears his hair long, below his shoulders, because (he says) long hair is beautiful and men should be permitted to be beautiful, too—beard— plays chess and competes in chess tournaments in Hamburg, Barcelona, etc.—eats health foods—while in Rome last year decided he needed a costume + had made for himself six silk turbans of different colors + six matching silk shirts plus a huge red velvet cloak, such as a carnival magician might wear . . .

J—late 20's, French, Jewish—has an illegitimate child— takes drugs (white powder in a bottle)—"Tell H in three months I go to Israel"—both parents died in concentration camp, she was hidden—saved by a Gentile family—loose black hair, large black eyes, black sweater, small body. Always drunk . . .

Herta Haussmann—German, painter (but not abstract)— atelier in Montparnasse with "chien mechant" in the yard below—Hungarian boyfriend Diorka . . .

Ricardo Vigón—Cuban; age 30; came to Paris 8–10 years ago; studied at the Cinemathèque 2 years, also wrote poetry; last two years has worked as a translator (into Spanish) at UNESCO. Had fervent religious period, + even lived for a short time in a monastery outside Paris. Fought against his homosexuality, then completely surrendered to it.

Elliott Stein—age 32 or so—from New York—Paris correspondent for *Opera* (published in London)—culture-vulture with recherché camp tastes—cinephile ("favorite movie": *King Kong*). Collects pornography.

Iris Owens—from New York, age 28, has written 5 pornos under name of "Harriet Daimler"—heavy black eye make-up (some carbon mixture)—once married . . . Brightest girl of her class at Barnard, thought she would go to Columbia Graduate School + study with [Lionel] Trilling. Boyfriend Takis (Greek sculptor).

Germán—another member of Cuban colony. Tall. Wife "Assumpsion" and son of five. Studied at Cinemathèque.

Sam Wolfenstein—Father a famous successful doctor + amateur classicist. Older brother big-shot physicist at Brookhaven . . . Fought in Israel in 1948—wounded—limps badly— never received compensation, hates Israel.

Allen Ginsberg—Hotel on rue Git-le-Coeur—boyfriend Peter [Orlovsky] with long blond hair + peak face.

H. Finest flower of American bohemia. New York. Family apartments in the 70s and 80s. Middle-class business (not professional) father. Communist aunts. Own history of CP [Communist Party] flirtation. Negro maid. New York high school, NYU, experimental artsy-craftsy college, San Francisco [*where she and SS first met*], flat in Greenwich Village. Early sexual experience, including Negroes. Homosexuality. Writes short stories. Bisexual promiscuity. Paris. Lives with a painter. Father moves to Miami. Trips back to America. Expatriate-type night employment. Writing peters out.

•

The rates [failures], the failed intellectuals (writers, artists, would-be Ph.Ds). People like Sam Wolfenstein [a mathematician], with his limp, his briefcase, his empty days, his addiction to films, his penny-pinching and scavengering, his arid family nest from which he flees—terrifies me.

12/30/57

My relationship to H baffles me. I want it to be unpremeditated, unreflective—but the shadow of her expectations about what an "affair" consists in upsets my poise, makes me fumble. She with her romantic dissatisfactions, I with my romantic need and longing . . . One unexpected gift: that she is beautiful. I had remembered her [ *from SS's days at Cal* ] as definitely not beautiful, rather gross and unattractive. She's anything but that. And physical beauty is enormously, almost morbidly, important to me.

*[Undated, late 1957]*

Moon a yellow smudge in the sky—a yellow fingerprint on the night.

•

Notes on Films

Voyeuristic intimacy of the camera.

The "belle image" theory of film—a film is a series
of beautiful images . . . vs. film as moving, entirely
integrated.

The camera, by moving around, subtly invites us
to embrace one character + exclude another; to look
up + feel awe of a hero or fear of a villain; to look
down + feel contempt or pity; a sidelong glance of
the camera alerts us for trouble; a right-to-left pan,
reversing the right handedness Hermann Weyl
discusses in his book on symmetry, invests people +
places with a spooky feeling.

The movie is the novel in motion; it is potentially
the least rationalistic, the most subjectivized
medium.

12/31/57

On Keeping a Journal.

Superficial to understand the journal as just a
receptacle for one's private, secret thoughts—like a
confidante who is deaf, dumb, and illiterate. In the
journal I do not just express myself more openly
than I could do to any person; I create myself.

The journal is a vehicle for my sense of selfhood.
It represents me as emotionally and spiritually
independent. Therefore (alas) it does not simply
record my actual, daily life but rather—in many
cases—offers an alternative to it.

There is often a contradiction between the meaning
of our actions toward a person and what we say we
feel toward that person in a journal. But this does
not mean that what we do is shallow, and only what
we confess to ourselves is deep. Confessions, I mean
sincere confessions of course, can be more shallow
than actions. I am thinking now of what I read
today (when I went up to 122 B[oulevar]d S[ain]t-
G[ermain] to check for her mail) in H's journal
about me—that curt, unfair, uncharitable assessment of me which concludes by her saying that she
really doesn't like me but my passion for her is
acceptable and opportune. God knows it hurts, and I
feel indignant and humiliated. We rarely do know
what people think of us (or, rather, think they think
of us) . . . Do I feel guilty about reading what was
not intended for my eyes? No. One of the main
(social) functions of a journal or diary is precisely to
be read furtively by other people, the people (like
parents + lovers) about whom one has been cruelly
honest only in the journal. Will H ever read this?

•

Writing. It's corrupting to write with intent to moralize, to
elevate people's moral standards.

Nothing prevents me from being a writer except laziness. A good writer.

Why is writing important? Mainly, out of egotism, I suppose. Because I want to be that persona, a writer, and not because there is something I must say. Yet why not that, too? With a little ego-building—such as the fait accompli this journal provides—I shall win through to the confidence that I (I) have something to say, that should be said.

My "I" is puny, cautious, too sane. Good writers are roaring egotists, even to the point of fatuity. Sane me, critics, correct them—but their sanity is parasitic on the creative faculty of genius.

# 1958

1/2/58

Poor little ego, how did you feel today? Not very well, I fear—rather bruised, sore, traumatized. Hot waves of shame, and all that. I never had any illusion she was in love with me, but I did assume she liked me.

•

Tonight (last night!) at Paul's place I reely wuz speeking French. For owers 'n 'owers, with him and his very sweet parents. What great fun!!

•

. . . Self-strategies.

How to make my sadness more than a lament for feeling? How to feel? How to burn? How to make my anguish metaphysical?

Blake says:

> If the Sun and Moon should Doubt
> They'd immediately go Out.

I am scared, numbed from the marital wars—that deadly, deadening combat which is the opposite, the antithesis of the sharp painful struggles of lovers. Lovers fight with knives and whips, husbands and wives with poisoned marshmallows, sleeping pills, and wet blankets.

*[What follows is in a journal whose cover is labeled Dec. 1957. It was almost certainly written in early 1958, though the month is unclear. It is a barely fictionalized account of SS's decision to leave her husband and how she wound up in Paris via Oxford. The persona in the story is called Lee—SS's middle name. Lee's husband is called Martin, the name of Philip Rieff's younger brother. Interestingly, the Paris lover otherwise modeled on H. is a man, called "Hazlitt," not a woman, and the figure representing Irene Fornes, who was to become SS's lover after H., is Hazlitt's Spanish lover, Maria. Reproduced here are SS's introduction to the account and its first part. In the early paragraphs I have melded a later version of Lee's decision to go to Europe into the body of the text, though in the notebook, it is added at the end.]*

*[Preface]*

The time for writing to entertain other people is over. I don't write to entertain others, or myself. This book is an instrument, a tool—and it must be hard + shaped like a tool, long, thick, and blunt.

This notebook is not a diary. It is not an aid to memory, so that I can remember that on such and such a date I saw that film of Buñuel, or how unhappy I was over J, or that Cádiz seemed beautiful but Madrid not.

*[Text]*

. . . She felt herself needing more and more sleep. When she awoke in the morning, she thought of when she might lie down again—after the morning teaching, or before the afternoon seminar—and when she would sleep.

She started going to the movies

In the sixth year of their marriage, Lee decided to come abroad for a year + applied for a scholarship to do it on. The plan was, as usual, joint. Martin was to come, too, but at the last moment he had a better offer for the year. She won her scholarship. He begged her not to go, but it was official and she had the progress of her career to hide behind. Otherwise she would never have had the guts to go. There was weeping and scenes and then suddenly it was time to go. There was a sleepless night in which she finally left their bed and went to sleep in the child's room, and then in the morning Martin and the child and the nurse drove away, and a few days later Lee went to New York and took a boat.

*[Alternate version of the decision to leave]*

"Martin, dear," Lee said one day, coming into his study, "I want to go away for a while." Martin was wearing his bathrobe over a tee-shirt and a pair of unpressed chino pants.

"Go where?" he answered, pushing the typewriter away from his knees.

"You know, travel—really travel—in Europe."

"But sweetheart, we've talked about this before. Next year, when the book is finished, we'll both apply for teaching positions abroad. It's all settled."

"But I can't wait!" she cried. "It's always next year, and next year, and nothing ever happens. And we sit in this rat hole on our asses growing eminent and middle-aged and paunchy—" She stopped, aware that it was no "we" she meant, and that this attack was entirely unprovoked.

She had been a feverish and gentle and weepy girl when she married Martin; now she was a shrewish, weak, tearless woman, full of premature bitterness . . . how Martin depended on her in his work . . .

*[Return to the first version]*

She knew a few people, publishers, university professors, in New York—acquaintances of Martin's and hers—but she never had a desire to see them when she was alone, so she let no one know she was in the city, and no one came to see her off on the boat. She rose late, almost missed the 11:00 sailing, however.

*[Alternate version of the departure]*

. . . She felt a savage desire to come to Europe, and all the myths of Europe echoed in her mind. Corrupt Europe, tired Europe, amoral Europe. She, who had been used to being precocious at twenty-four felt stupidly lumpishly innocent, and she wanted that innocence to be violated.

I have lived in a dream of innocence, she whispered to herself, as she watched the wrinkled moon-spattered ocean night after night on the boat.

My innocence makes me weep.

I am a patient, she said. I am physician and patient at once. But self-knowledge is not the remedy I prescribe to myself. I want as much self-knowledge as I can get—let me not be deceived—but self-knowledge isn't the goal I seek. Strength, strength is what I want. Strength not to endure, I have that and it has made me weak—but strength to act—

*[Return to the first version]*

She went first to England and spent a lonely exhilarating term at a university, mixing with undergraduates, doing little work, rediscovering—as if she were sixteen—the fun of flirtations and living alone. But the atmosphere was too much like the one she'd known in America—the tense careerism of the academic world, the talkativeness of it. She felt sick of talk, of books, of intellectual industry, of the inhibited gate of the professor.

In December she went to Paris for the vacation, intending to return to Oxford in six weeks, but she never returned, and fell into a love affair in Paris as simply and without reservations as she had simply and without compromise denied her sexual need for so many years. The man in Paris was everything that Martin was not: he did not love her, and he was altogether lacking in physical or verbal tenderness. But she accepted this for the sake of their love-making which was violent, thoroughly sexual, not sticky with personality.

Ah, she thought, I'm sick of the old melting giving yielding egos—my own included; and she made great and generous allowances for her lover's indifference.

This lover in Paris was also an American, who had lived there for almost a decade—himself an escaped intellectual, and deeply anti-intellectual. He had come to Paris to paint, but now painted very little but still lived in that world, and his mistresses had been painters or sculptors . . .

. . . Hazlitt talked all the time of his former mistress, a Spanish painter named Maria—voluptuous, primitive, and magically sensitive. They had been lovers for three years, although they had only for short periods lived together. She had left him and Paris three months before Judith came [*here Lee is changed to Judith, also the name of SS's younger sister*], and he was still violently and sentimentally in love with her . . .

[*The text simply ends in the middle of the story, after which there is only the following note.*] sexualization of life, seeing the world through a trope in this case, sexual attraction, sexual adventure, sexual failure

1/2/58

. . . My emotional life: dialectic between craving for privacy and need to submerge myself in a passionate relationship to another. Note—with Philip I have *neither*, neither privacy nor passion. Neither the heightening of self which is only won by privacy and loneliness, nor the splendid heroic beautiful loss of self that accompanies passion.

More reasons for doing You Know What. But reason won't make me do it, only will.

1/3/58

I pass this day by, as too painful + problematic for comment. Seven years is a long time, isn't it, dear one? A life-time, indeed. I have given you my youth, my weakness, my hopes. I have taken from you your masculinity, your self-confidence, your strength—but not (alas) your hopes.

1/4/58

Last night, an incredible film, *Les Maîtres fous* about the Haouka cult (1927–   ) in Accra. The world as dramatic representation. The image of a dead ceremonious civilization seen through a fantastic naïve *vivant* barbarism . . . With this African film, the Swedish *La Nuit des forains.* The long silent sequence at the beginning is surely one of the most intense + beautiful things in the history of the cinema— ranking a little below the Odessa Steps sequence in *Potemkin.* The rest of the film rather an anti-climax, though very good. Wonderful close-ups of the actor's face + the girls.

•

*[On Paris]*

*The city.* The city as labyrinth. (No labyrinths in the country.) This, among other things, attracts me.

The city is vertical. The country (+ suburbs) horizontal.

I "set myself" in the city . . .

The arts of the city: signs, advertising, buildings, uniforms, non-participant spectacles.

The city is based on the principle that the seasons (Nature) don't, needn't matter. Hence, automatic air-conditioning, central heating, the taxi, etc. The city has no seasons but it provides a sharper contrast between day + night than the country. The city overcomes night (with artificial lighting + artificial sociability in bars, restaurants, parties), it *uses* night—as night remains unused, is a negative time in the country.

Important development: with the coming of automobiles, the banishing of animals from the city, what must cities have been like suffused with the stench of horse dung?

Trees growing out of the pavement. Dead nature, circumscribed, trimmed. The asphalt playground.

The policeman guide to the labyrinth, as much as guardian of civic order.

The limits of urban sociability. Privacy (vs. solitude) as a distinctively urban creation.

The sky, as seen in the city, is negative—where the buildings are not.

•

Duty, Responsibility. These words *do* mean something to me. Yet, once I admit that *I have* duties, am I not inexorably committed to considering them as opposed to my inclinations? Can I recognize that I have duties, without knowing what these are? Can I recognize what these duties are, without discharging them?

To understand the world is to view it outside of one's sentiments. This is the natural difference between understanding and acting, though this difference can be erased—as by Gide in his notion of the "acte gratuit."

I water my white mind with books.

Impenetrable disorder of human relations.

H finds my virtues defects. [*Originally, SS wrote "vices," then crossed it out.*] (I'm not interesting enough to have vices.) Putting aside all explanation by way of her own confusions and defensiveness, is it possible? E.g., consider the phenomenon of honesty. *Why* be honest? Why this lust to expose oneself, to become transparent? Detestable, if it stems from the need to claim *pity* from others.

Sense of reality = sense that things must be as they are. (Spinoza, Stoics) In me, very therapeutic but premature. I've had the cure before ever having had the disease.

Price of freedom is unhappiness. I must distort my soul to write, to be free.

•

Nominalist attitude to objects in pre-cubist painting.

Kandinsky doesn't stand up very well compared with Klee. (Show of Kandinsky's watercolors + gouaches, 1927–1940, last Saturday afternoon at the Galerie Maeght, with H.) But, interesting: premonitions + anticipations of distinctively XXth-century shapes: the geometry of television aerials, missile launching sites, entrails of machinery (more subtle than Léger); satellite orbits + cosmic space . . .

•

Katharine Hepburn—hair drawn back, lean, even bony figure; tailored clothes with high-necked blouses; decisive manners; forthright-shy grin;—is the incarnation of the feminist ideal of a woman. (Interesting that she has always been Philip's favorite Hollywood actress.) If exemplary independent women, images of femisinism, are homosexuals— Garbo, Hepburn, de Beauvoir (so Annette [Michelson, film critic and scholar] reported today)—does this undermine the feminist case?

•

H returns tomorrow. I feel desperately sad, sick with the expectation that it will be over. She didn't write. Tonight, at the start of *Les Enfants du Paradis* (which I saw at the Bonaparte [cinema], where the music begins very loudly, nakedly melodic—I was on the verge of bursting into violent tears. The first time in months that I've felt capable of weeping . . .

Through the music, I recalled—condensed—the great sadness of the film. The chain of unfulfilled love: W loves X, but X loves Y, and Y, Y loves Z. "I love you," says Nathalie to Baptiste Debureau, "and you love Garance, and Garance loves Frédérick." "What makes you say that?" shouts Baptiste. "They live together." "Ah," replies Baptiste, "if all the people who lived together loved each other, the earth would shine like the sun!"

I can already envisage H's brittle demonstrativeness, my own gaucherie—my idiotic attempts to elicit her love. Suffocating *not* to talk, to make things clear; suicidal to talk, causing her either to lie (what she's been doing) or to be honest.

Will she say tomorrow night (tonight!) on the 'phone, when I call her at the *Herald Trib* before theatre with Paul, that she's tired from her trip + would rather go directly home? I can hear myself saying, after a slight pause (it *can't* be as wretched as that first night alone, that second Monday night in Paris), sure, of course, I understand . . . NO, I won't say that. I won't tamely agree. If she asks if I mind, I intend to say that I *do*, that I mind very much . . .


1/6/58

H back; games of sex, love, friendship, banter, melancholy resumed. Tells of a whorish, splendid time in Dublin. Christ, she's beautiful! and hard to be with, even on the plane of her own duplicity. Egotistical, edgy, mocking, bored with me, bored with Paris, bored with herself.

We've taken a high-ceilinged white room in [Grand] Hôtel de l'Univers, rue Grégoire de Tours, for the next nine days.

•

*Henri IV* of Pirandello last night with Paul + civil servant friends. (TNP [Théâtre National Populaire]: Jean Vilar)

Despite the fact that I could only understand about half the French, + that I was sick, literally sick in the pit of my stomach, with anxiety about my meeting with H at 12:00, I had emotional room to be profoundly moved by the play again. Pirandello's schmaltzy reflections on illusion & reality have always appealed to me.* I liked too the bright, aggressive staging; the simple harlequin-type costumes (blue + green, red + yellow, red + blue, green + yellow for the four courtiers; all red for the emperor); but not so much the acting—except for Vilar, who would make a splendid Richard II, by the way. French acting in the theatre—this is not so true in the films, where a sort of international "realist" style prevails—is very florid + extravagant. The actor begins on a highly stylized emphatic level—and must top that, often becoming a little hysterical, to represent a violent emotion.

No mask is wholly a mask. Writers and psychologists have explored the face-as-mask. Not so well appreciated: the mask-as-face. Some people, no doubt, do wear their masks as a sheathe for the lithe but insupportable emotions beneath. But surely most people wear a mask to efface what is beneath and become only what the mask represents them to be.

More interesting than the mask as concealment or disguise is the mask as projection, as aspiration. Through the mask of my behavior, I do not protect my raw genuine self—I overcome it.

•

Saturday afternoon's long semi-drunk conversation with Annette Michelson, mostly about marriage. I was trying to

---

*In 1979, SS would direct Pirandello's As You Desire Me at the Teatro Stabile di Torino.

describe P's innocence to her, and instanced how he's urged me to spend only a short while in Oxford + the balance of the year in Paris. "Go to Paris, it must be great fun." Annette immediately understood, + replied: "He doesn't know, then, he's cutting his own throat."

•

Dreamt last night of a beautiful, mature David of about eight years, to whom I talked, eloquently and indiscreetly, about my own emotional stalemates as Mother used to talk to me—when I was nine, ten, eleven . . . He was so sympathetic and I felt great peace in explaining myself to him.

I hardly ever dream of David, and don't think of him much. He has made few inroads on my fantasy-life. When I am with him, I adore him completely and without ambivalence. When I go away, as long as I know he's well taken-care-of, he dwindles very quickly. Of all the people I have loved, he's least of all a *mental* object of love, most intensely real.

•

TNP building is like what one imagines a Soviet Palace of Rest and Culture to be like. Immense, vulgar, expensively-built, with marble walls and little glass, huge staircases and escalators, fantastically high ceilings, brass railings and gigantesque murals. It's the biggest theatre in Paris, Paul says. After the play, + before I go to meet H, we stood in the great plaza between the flanks of the Palais de Chaillot, looking toward the Eiffel Tower which is planted straight ahead in an unobstructed view—the Tower heroically big + black and perfectly articulated against a beautiful night sky of restless white clouds and generous moonlight.

1/7/58

H extremely distant, hostile, self-absorbed.

Reflections on hell, occasioned by the visually superb, musically so-so *Don Giovanni* I saw at the Opéra last night. Idea of hell & idea that the universe has a garbage can, an automatic disposal unit. Hell seemed *just* to R.C.'s, Calvinists; *uncharitable* to latter-day Protestants. Is the insistence on justice (judging) dissolved by the claim of charity?

Idea of an afterlife, including hell, demanded by religious teleology? Moral bookkeeping requires a settling of accounts. Some enterprises prosper, others are judged bankrupt or fraudulent or both—and there must be penalties + rewards, for life is *serious*. It's easy to see how the virtue of justice, + the arts + scruples of judging, go with a serious attitude toward life—less easy to see that charity is serious, because so much of behavior which is objective [*sic*] charitable stems from indifference and an incapacity for moral indignation.

I remember a talk with Herbert Hart last spring in Cambridge [Mass.] (standing before Schoenhof's on Mass. Ave., after a lecture of his) about the Nuremberg trials, which he cut off by saying, "I don't go in much for judging myself." It seemed absurd, indecent!

I suppose it's very Protestant to think that religion must be serious, or it's not really religion. There is the gaiety of the Chassidim, the aestheticism + muddle of Hindu ritual which [E. M.] Forster describes.

Seriousness is really a virtue for me, one of the few which [I] accept existentially and will emotionally. I love being gay and forgetful, but this only has meaning against the background imperative of seriousness.

1/8/58

What I lack [*SS had originally written "want," then crossed it out*], as a writer, is (1) inventiveness, and (2) the power to sustain an exact sense. H went to her room today after we got up, before lunch. Spent the late afternoon exploring the Sorbonne, + the pre-dinner hour seeing [the Marx Brothers'] *Monkey Business* at the Celtic.

A torrent (five!) of letters—piteous, tender, sentimental— from Philip waiting for me today at American Express.

1/9/58

P has been fired at Brandeis, and I hardly know what to feel. Relief at not being with him + having to coach, exhort, comfort . . . Compassion for the anxieties he must be suffering . . . A slight feeling of fear at the way my so solid-seeming life seems to be breaking up beneath my feet—everything urging me to decide, to act, to leave him when I go back.

With H, it seems to go better—but then, I *can't* know, and I was very wrong before, about the pre-Dublin weeks.

Yesterday, dinner (Charpentier) + [Racine's] *Britannicus* ([at the Théâtre du] Vieux Colombier with Annette Michelson, who was more arch + artificial than usual. She doesn't like H at all, and therefore I don't like her. Racine is more foreign than the Kabuki plays—emotions are externalized, mathematical. The play consists of a series of confrontations of two or at most three characters (no Shakespearean waste!); the intellectual medium is neither dialogue nor soliloquy, but something in-between, which I found unpleasing—the tirade. No movement, just postures.

Marguerite Jamois, who was Agrippine, looks very grand + stagey—a sort of ideal Edith Sitwell.

H agonizingly late last night. She was to come directly to the room, and didn't arrive until 2:15 . . . I stood at the window + stared down into the narrow street, watching a beggar, two cats, a man who paced about + finally stood in the doorway next to the "cremerie," waiting for someone—and listening to footsteps, which for an hour + a half, weren't hers.

1/12/58

H having just gone to work, I've returned to the hotel to change before meeting Irving Jaffe at the Old Navy [café] at 7:30. H is beautiful, relaxed, affectionate. I—dizzy with passion and need for her, and happy . . . good god, I *am* happy! I suppose, with my sore heart + unused body, it doesn't take much to make me happy. Yet that's *not* all, and I do both her and myself an injustice to say that. It's she, it's she, it's she.

Friday night, a mediocre *Der Rosenkavalier*, I, alone, riding the crest of erotic fantasy, the tide of the familiar gorgeous music . . . Met H at the [Café] Flore afterwards, and had 5 or so whiskeys at the Club St. Germain and the Tabou. Not stupefied drunk, but enough to get with the so-so jazz we were hearing at the St. Germain, and with the superb sex we had near dawn, in bed.

I'd already decided to get drunk in the late afternoon, after the news from America. Had a drink in a Champs-Élysées bar before we went to a film, *L'Alibi*, with [Erich] Von Stroheim, [Louis] Jouvet, + Roger Blin. Then I walked in the rain to the Opéra, skipping dinner.

Saturday, yesterday, we slept late, ate at the Greek's next door, waited briefly for Ricardo at the Old Navy, picked up the radio + shoes. H ordered a pair of pants; then she went on to a [*Herald*] *Tribune* cocktail party + I to a couple of unscheduled hours with Han (I don't like him) and Monique (I don't get her at all). Met H in her room at nine. Great meal at the Beaux-Arts. An hour to collect people—Paola + Bruno, Han + Monique—+ then we drove to the later, more "serious" *Tribune* party. Bruno was absurd, and almost spoiled it. That dumpy, over-dressed blonde, Hilary—sort-of-friend of H's—made a big pass at me, which I liked a lot. I wasn't attracted to her, but it was so good to be home, as it were—to have women, instead of men, interested in me . . . As we left, Han stole a chair . . . Oh, and Monique + I had a big soulish conversation about sex, love, women, men, her husband, my lover . . .

Slept until 3:00 today. Vile sandwich at the Old Navy. Awful people who joined us—Diego, Evelyn, Londyn. H looked especially lovely this evening, dressed and on her way to the *Tribune*.

2/8/58

Time to break this silence—Somehow, this journal had become charmed, au fond I felt it destined to record real bonheur, and when everything came crashing, the day of my birthday when we moved into the Hôtel de Poitou, the impulse to write in it expired.

What happened, the total collapse of my affair with H, was so sudden I couldn't believe it was what it appeared to be. Wednesday night—[Chaplin's] *Modern Times*, and her being early, there at midnight, at the Flore, and going to the Club 55, and her presents waiting for me in the room, and above all, her really being tender and *with* me—was so beautiful; I was filled with joy—not deceiving myself that she loved me as I love her, but thinking that she was a little happy in our relationship, that she liked me, that we were good together. Thursday, we moved—and Thursday night, at Lapérouse and the theatre ([Luigi Pirandello's] *Ce soir on improvise*) was a kind of hell such as I've rarely been through. I felt myself blindly walking through a forest of pain, my inner eyes clenched shut, trying to keep from weeping. (Almost did at Lapérouse.) Then Friday, Saturday, Sunday in this hotel, + more of the same—with me dumb, stupefied like an animal, with pain—and she, riding me all the time for being moody, selfish, temperamental, a drag . . .

Sunday afternoon, the walk to the l'Île St. Louis—Sunday night, a lurching, snow-whipped, glamorous plane-ride to London—and then that crazy week of preparation for my return to France, in which I was neither here (in Paris) nor there emotionally, but suspended—still incredulous.

Sunday night—Jan. 26—I returned, an endless dull flight it seemed, hauled my suitcases up to the room—it was already 1:30 a.m.—to find H as before, and myself so despairing and sad I couldn't kiss her. I had had the curse the four days before I left, she had had it four, five days (she led me to understand) after my return. No sex, and worse still, the way she moves her body away from any touch of mine in bed . . .

Since then, it's thirteen days since my return, we've made love three or four times—once this past Monday night, very beautifully. Once since then. Every afternoon she works in her room at 226 Blvd. S[t.] G[ermain].

It's Saturday night, she's at dinner with friends, the host, someone named Sidney Leach, is responsible for getting her this translation job, so she can quit the *Tribune*. Ten o'clock. I am to meet her at 11:00 at the Old Navy.

Haven't had dinner. Reading [Italo Svevo's novel] *The Confessions of Zeno*, which moves and impresses me deeply.

•

Let me say it once more to myself. It's over. In the real sense: not that H no longer loves me, for she never did, but that she no longer plays the game of love. She didn't love, but we *were* lovers. We aren't any longer, haven't been since moving into this goddam hotel room, seething with her ghosts, with her memories of Irene [Fornes]. What sickens me is that she's come to dislike me, really, and doesn't at all feel required to hide it. She's openly rude, as when she hurried out slamming the door in my face, at the Beaux-Arts Friday after our lunch there. Insults, shoves, grimaces. And not a word of affection, not a single embrace or handclasp or look of tenderness. In short, she finds our relationship absurd, neither liking nor sexually desiring me anymore. And indeed it is absurd.

. . . A crucifixion, these last two weeks . . . Must deserve it. Love is ridiculous. Feel continuously flushed + dizzy: actually did run a fever late Tuesday night and stayed in bed— with some provisions brought up by H before she went off at noon—all day Wednesday.

Mon coeur blessé . . .

And Thursday afternoon, I was invited up to her room, Irene's room, (*both* rooms are hers, and Irene's) to help out, editing, the translation. Oh God, I don't want to remember! And that night, walking in the snow—so hot, so hot—and meeting Hilary + John Flint + then the racket of the Monaco, and our rendez-vous at 12:30 at the Deux Magots— so blind + love-sick and gut-torn I could barely stand.

Yesterday was better, all afternoon with Monique + Irving—I really forgot a bit, stepped outside my bloody wreck of a self in the intellectual effort of speaking French. But afterwards! H engaged in introspection and counsel à la St. Germain des Prés with her friend Reggie. And that unspeakable "party" in Passy from 4–6 . . .

Face up to things, kid. You've had it . . .

•

H thinks she is decadent because she has entered into a relation which neither physically nor emotionally interests her. How decadent then am I, who know how she really feels, and still want her?

". . . they find . . . that this lover has committed the unpardonable error of not being able to exist—and they come down with a dummy in their arms." (*Nightwood*)

2/15/58

I don't know whether I feel better, or I've become numb. But there is peace in being sure, even in being sure of some great fatality or refusal. I think I feel better. I look at everything from the other end—instead of expecting all and being lowered into despair each time I get less, I expect nothing now and, occasionally, I get a little, and am more than a little happy.

•

Gave H Nathanael West's *Collected Works*, and have started *The Dream Life of Balso Snell*, which is funny and painful and very fine. Finished *Zeno*.

•

P in New York, looking for a job, ineptly. I find it increasingly tedious to write, have stopped writing daily, carry crumpled half-written letters around in the pocket of my donkey coat for days.

The thought of going back to my old life—it hardly even seems like a dilemma any more. I can't, I won't. I can say that now without strain.

The dropper and the dropped, the tombeuse and the tombé. How hard to thrust my hand through the cobweb curtain. All those years, and I couldn't do it, I didn't have the will.

And now, it's so easy—I'm already on the other side from which it's impossible to return.

Marriage is a sort of tacit hunting in couples. The world all in couples, each couple in its own little house, watching its own little interests + stewing in its own little privacy—it's the most repulsive thing in the world. One's got to get rid of the *exclusiveness* of married love.

2/19/58

H said something very striking yesterday, apropos of Sam W.'s enormous library, that collecting books in that way was "like marrying someone in order to sleep with him."

True . . .

Use libraries!!

We have taken the Wolfenstein apartment for two months— I still can't imagine why she wants to live with me, feeling as she does . . .

. . . Yesterday (late afternoon) I went to my first Paris cock-tail party, at Jean Wahl's [*1888–1974, Professor of Philosophy at the Sorbonne*]—in the disgusting company of Allan Bloom. Wahl very much lived up to my expectations—a tiny slim birdlike old man with lank white hair and wide thin mouth, rather beautiful, like Jean-Louis Barrault will be at 65, but terribly *distrait* and unkempt. Baggy black suit with three large holes in the rear end through which you could see his (white) underwear, + he'd just come from a late afternoon lecture—on [Paul] Claudel—at the Sorbonne. Has a tall handsome Tunisian wife (with a round face and tightly-drawn-back black hair) half his age, about 35–40 I'd guess, + three or four quite young children. Also there were Giorgio de Santillana [*historian of science at MIT*]; two Japanese artists; lean old ladies in fur hats; a man from [the magazine] *Preuves*; middle-sized children straight out of Balthus, in Mardi Gras costumes; a man who looked like Jean-Paul Sartre; and lots of other people whose names meant nothing to me. I talked to Wahl and de Santillana + (unavoidably) to Bloom. The apartment, it's in the rue Peletier, is fantastic—all the walls are drawn + sketched + painted on by the children and by artist friends—there is dark carved North African furniture, ten thousand books, heavy tablecloths, flowers, paintings, toys, fruit—a rather beautiful disorder, I thought.

2/20/58

Of this unshy Jewish pornographer s'appele [*sic*] Harriet Daimler: "She's a hipster. She doesn't get hung up."

My mind eludes me. I have to surprise it from behind, in the act of talking.

The nights are the worst. The torment of lying, sleepless, beside the body one uniquely desires, and not being able to break through, to command desire in return. Side by side. Or like spoons. Be careful not to touch! Awful awful feeling of "déjà été," for I did desire Philip tremendously during the first year.

I mind H's physical rejection of me most of all, most by far. At this point I'd accept any attitude, any assessment of me—even fervent dislike—if there were sexual warmth between us. But without that, am I not *indeed* being masochistic in continuing to live with her? What price love? I don't like at all the role I've fallen into, nor do I like her brand of frivolous sadism. Several times in the past days I've been on the verge of shaking her by the shoulders. I want to slap her—not to annihilate or to efface (which is the meaning behind *her* shoves and pokes at me) but to force her really to regard me, with hate if need be, force her to end this stupidity of living with hearts and bodies averted . . .

•

"Have I not shut my eyes with the added shutter of the night and put my hand out? And it's the same with girls, those who turn the day into night, the young, the drug addict, the profligate, the drunken and that most miserable, the lover who watches all night long in fear and anguish. These can never again live the life of the day . . ."

(*Nightwood*)

•

2/21/58

[Brecht's] *The Caucasian Chalk Circle* in a somewhat Pirandello-ized production, last night (with Paul): I liked the effect of stylization—the music (drum, cymbals, flute, guitar) with its crude underlining of the action; the shiny two-thirds-length masks which just cover the upper lip and thus exaggerate the mouth; the tilted stage and casual props (the actors bring their own props on stage, as in the Chinese theatre), the device of the narrator and the general charm of dédoublement, of the play-within-a-play . . .

Pirandello, Brecht, Genet—for all three, in exemplary and contrasting ways, the subject of the theatre is—the theatre. As for Action Painters, the subject of painting is the painter's act. Compare [Pirandello's] *Ce soir on improvise*, [Genet's] *Les Bonnes, The Caucasian Chalk Circle* . . . For me this is the interest of Brecht, even though his plots are of a deliberately folk-like childish simplicity, and he *purports* to be teaching his audience, about the world, justice, etc.

Genet's new play, the one he's revising now, uses—and is all about—screens. The characters draw on screens, attach things to them, project their secret characters while at the same time engaging in a "realistic" action. A new, visual, version of the soliloquy . . .

The screen + the mask, as blackboard.

I don't like didactic plays. But I like philosophical, playful plays.

Psychological plays? There's a more difficult issue. Perhaps the French are right in disliking psychological plays, psychological novels, psychology—in the Anglo-American and German manner—in general.

The ideal of plays in which psychological insight is entirely exteriorized, cf. Artaud: ". . . Il s'agit donc, pour le théâtre, de créer une métaphysique de la parole, du geste, de l'expression, en vue de l'arracher à son piétinement psychologique et humain."

2/23/58

Chez Wolfenstein—feeling of an immense, intolerable burden having been lifted. H, whom I love—is beautiful, beautiful. Can she? Will she want to be a little happy with me here? . . . We came here yesterday afternoon, and ate, and danced to Ricardo [Vigón's] record, and went out in the evening with the Italians (Terry, Pia) to the Trois Fontaines and after to the [Café de] Tournon. At the Tournon: H's drunken grace, talking, laughing, playing the pinball machines; Han; that Israeli who flirted with me; the Negro has a date with [blank] for Tuesday . . .

. . . My ambition—or my consolation—has been to *understand* life. (Mistaken idea of the spirituality of a writer?) Now I want simply to learn to live with it. Among other things, H's extraordinary destructive self-consciousness and consciousness-of-others teaches me this. From this, her flair for satiety . . .

I tried to say this yesterday—the day before?—but as usual didn't succeed. She always takes issue with my ideas, with what she takes to be my intellectuality. She assumes *she's* the anti-intellectual.

"mouth-hungry, not stomach-hungry . . ."

2/25/58

An evening of reading, dutiful letter-writing, of privacy and equilibrium.

Joanne Chatelin here this afternoon. Before she came I Métro'd to American Express to pick up mail. Haven't been for two weeks—the longest interval by far. Along with an accelerating delinquency in my writing of letters to Philip is a growing reluctance, aversion even, to collect and read his to me. But today's batch contained the bright surprise of his almost certain appointment at Berkeley. How clear-cut that will make my own decision. I shall be able to make no excuses to myself—

Thinking much of P:—of his timidity, his sentimentality, his low vitality, his innocence. There is a type—the male virgin—lots of them in England, I suppose. He cares so fiercely for his domestic sanctuary, for David and me, so little for anyone else—Since I broke the spell of pity and dependence that bound him to his parents. Such a life, such a temperament, is not easily repaired when damaged. P is a bleeder, in fact physically, and emotionally, too. He won't die of this grief but neither will he ever recover from it.

•

To be defensive invites, incites the other person to offend. Remember!! X looks abjectly-lovingly at Y; Y is irritated by mounting self-reproaches, which are resented as being undeserved; therefore Y feels compelled to be brutal to X.

Sadism, hostility an essential element in love. Therefore it's important that love be a *transaction* of hostilities.

Lesson: not to surrender one's heart where it's not wanted.

2/26/58

Capricorn [*SS's astrological sign*] prefers friendship to a tepid unpassionate love-affair. That was H's gift to me last night in the Tabou, proffered with a broad grin . . .

Capricorn prefers neither. Has got neither. Detests both.

How *does* it apply, H? Perhaps to you? But not at all to me.

•

Your insatiability, dear H, that's just the consoling way in which your talent for satiety appears to you. Never to get what one wants *is* never to want (for long) what one gets— unless, sometimes, when it is taken away.

2/26/58

. . . Heard Simone de Beauvoir talk on the novel (is it still possible) last night at the Sorbonne (with Jaffe). She is lean and tense and black-haired and very good-looking for her age, but her voice is unpleasant, something about the high pitch + the nervous speed with which she talks—

In the late afternoon read Carson McCullers' *Reflections in a Golden Eye*. Slick, really economical and "written," but I don't go for motivation by apathy, catatonia, animal empathy . . . (In a novel, I mean!)

2/27/58

Beautiful concert at the Sorbonne tonight—Brandenburg [Concerto] # 6, Beethoven Violin Concerto (Georges Tessier), 2 Mozart arias ("Dalla sua pace" + one other), + the *Coronation* Mass # 15.

. . . "This false and dangerous relationship." More false, more dangerous for me than for H. It's real for me. For her, just an unsatisfying appearance she keeps up with a quarter of her attention—while she mourns for her Irene.

Reading Emma Goldman, *Living My Life* . . .

3/1/58

The nadir of my relation with H. The fantastic brutal insult of her love-making Thursday night—total estrangement yesterday . . . Did I know what was wrong? I should ask myself a few questions, etc., etc. I fled, weeping, into the Métro at 4:00—plunged into a movie (*Grand Hotel*, Garbo, Crawford); back to the Old Navy for a rendez-vous with Monique, Han there too; dinner at the Gaudeamus, getting drunk on slivovitz, not hearing, literally, any more; back to the Champs-Élysées for another film (*Témoin à charge* [*Witness for the Prosecution*])—still couldn't hear, or attend; got into the Métro at midnight with Han + Monique, + then foolishly shamelessly rushed out at Concorde to take a taxi to the Old Navy, where I'd said I'd be—hoping she would, knowing she wouldn't, be there . . .

3/24/58

Stop reserving this journal so exclusively for the chronology of my affair with H! Image of an image of image . . . It is enough—or rather, too much—that I love her, that I have enormous pleasure simply in looking at her, that once in a great while we make love, and well . . . But to record all the dips and upswings, in a sense falsifies them, and I start deluding myself and thinking all this is, or might be, real. Enough to play the game, or try to play it. A mistake to tally up the score . . .

. . . We get along, when we do get along, only when she—or both of us—is drunk. As she had to be drunk that Sunday early morning, three weeks ago, when she + I and Paula + Jerry came back here and got into bed and she struck me on the face and clawed my back and shouted that she hated me + I disgusted her, and I sobbed and tried to hit back and couldn't really . . . And then for five days everything was okay, and we were lovers again, as we hadn't been since December in Vidal's room—but by the end of the week, by the time of the party on March 8, it was over. The bruise on my face paled and finally disappeared, and so did the sexual warmth between us, and the rare juncture of our imaginations. It flared up once again the next day, at Marie-Pierre's soiree and then died down for good.

•

. . . An incredible film, Stroheim's *Foolish Wives*, at the Cinemathèque last night. A Don Juan film, with Stroheim's beautiful lascivious looks and gorgeous military-sexy costumes and sadistic manners. Salaciousness not a subject acknowledged in American films—and this man was [D. W.] Griffith's assistant!

4/15/58

After two weeks in Spain (Madrid, Seville, Cádiz, Tangiers) I am back in Paris . . . Why didn't I take this journal along? Because I knew H was taking hers, and it seemed so grotesque, the vision of the 2 of us sharing some hotel room writing before each other—manufacturing our private selves, coloring in our private hells—

Things were both better + worse than I expected—We neither quarreled (except for that absurd day in Seville when after she had made love to me in the afternoon, my face betrayed me, my despair + sense of being totally rejected, and she chose to take it as a rejection of her) nor were really close . . . I couldn't rid myself of the awareness of her unhappiness, of how Spain and speaking Spanish brought back her life with Irene. We were ceremonious and very separate . . .

. . . The corrida of Seville, the way my guts turned over when the first bull dropped to the sand. Tuesday in Madrid, the way the Bosch paintings and the flamenco music seethed all night in my head . . . The Nazi-style helmets on the soldiers who marched in some of the processions in Seville.

My left heel hurting, lacerated from the new shoes I bought the day before we left—the tapas bar off the Carrera San Jerónimo—the nightmare 3rd class train ride to Seville with 6 filthy, obscene Spanish "vitelloni" ("Norman Mailer," "The Clerk," "Clark Gable," "The Fat Friend," the rugged at the other window seat with the "bota" [wineskin])—

Waiting on the Triana bridge Saturday afternoon for the "paso" [*wooden float used in Holy Week processions*] which never came—Feeling hungry all the time, I guess because I was anxious and continually doubtful about whether I should have come and eager + sad + enjoying myself all at once—an unsettling mélange of feelings . . .

Buying sneakers late Wednesday afternoon in Madrid—The smell of incense & popcorn during the processions.

Cádiz was the most beautiful city I saw in Spain—the center very clean and modern with a hush of beautiful-sad poverty along the sea wall. A city of handsome but modest plazas, many narrow pedestrian streets, children and sailors, and the sea, and sun.

—Our walks along the sea wall, and the barelegged children who followed us.

—The plump young waiter in the restaurant our first night in Cádiz who wanted to make a date with H.

—Riding in a horse-drawn carriage to our hotel.

The bus ride from Cádiz to Algeciras when H told me of the nickname ("Pup" from Pulpo) that Irene + she had for each other—then was angry with me + herself for revealing this intimacy.

Eating crevettes in the quay café at Algeciras . . .

H being annoyed with me because I was excited on the boat over seeing Gibraltar.

. . . The lesbian couple in Tangier—Sandy, blond thin collegiate-looking butch, and Mary, big nose and large breasts, Portuguese.

. . . The brown leather wallet stamped with gold [that] H bought in the Socco—Drinking mint tea + listening to three Arab musicians who squatted in the center of the floor, in the café in the Sultan's palace.

The smells of Seville—incense and popcorn and jasmine and "churros."

4/20/58

Banality and domination—that's what I wrote back in U-Conn [*when SS was teaching there some years earlier*], and was right . . .

An aristocracy of sensibility as well as an aristocracy of intellect. Don't like at all, at all being treated as a plebeian!

Have to have enough ego to support my sensibility. If I were sensitive (i.e., showed my awareness of H's moods, what she really thinks of me), I'd *never* dare to embrace her . . .

Being in love—this subtle keen unforgettable sense of the other's uniqueness. There is no one like her, dances like her, is sad like her, is eloquent like her, is foolish and vulgar like her . . .

I tire of Barbara's presence. I love H too passionately, too sexually not to resent—more and more—this three sisters, tall girl club act, even though Barbara's *presence* diverts H + perhaps makes her less impatient with me.

4/26/58

Sick, feverish, losing my grip on myself. This passion is a disease! Just when I think I am regaining my control, recovering myself, it rises up and gives me a wallop below the belt . . . I've been *thinking* that I was less in love with H; certainly this affair corrupts me, and her continual attacks on my sense of self—be it my taste in food (remember that day in Seville, walking down Sierpes, after I'd had an almond drink, when she announced I had an "unrefined sensibility") or art or people, my public behavior, my sexual need— offends my love. I tell myself that she is destroying my love for her, by her hostility and vulgarity, that I need only let it happen, and I shall find myself sadly free. But it's not so . . .

4/27/58

Read Hemingway, *Torrents of Spring*; [Ivan Goncharov's] *Oblomov*; [Oscar Wilde's] *De Profundis*,

> "All trials are trials for one's life, just as all sentences are sentences of death." (Wilde)

5/31/58

What feelings I had seeing "Dachau, 7 km" as we sped along the Autobahn toward Munich in the Dutch anti-Semite's car!

•

A passive activity, an active passivity.

Me to H: "It's rather that you're bored with *yourself.* You can't build your life around emotional and sexual tourism. You need a vocation . . ."

Tourism essentially a passive activity. You set yourself in a certain surrounding—expecting to be excited, amused, entertained. You need bring nothing to the situation—the surrounding is sufficiently charged.

Tourism and boredom.

6/1/58

Munich.

Sky cobbled with clouds.

The poetry of ruins.

Wide, empty, asphalt streets; cream-colored anonymous new buildings; fat-necked, fat-assed American soldiers on the prowl in their long pastel cars.

The Frauenkirche with its two breast-towers.

7/4/58

What difference could there be between the situation of one person who was sane while all the rest of the world was mad, and that of one person who was mad while everyone else was sane?

None.

Their situations are the same. Madness and sanity the same, in isolation.

6/25/58

*[This entry is accompanied by a sketched self-portrait of SS lying down.]*

... *Not* to look at abstract paintings for the shapes—scenes—one can discern in them. That is to look at painting in a literary rather than a plastic way. But then one can *say* little or nothing about them . . .

7/4/58

Read, since returning from Germany: [Alberto] Moravia, *A Ghost at Noon* + Faulkner, *Sanctuary*. Re-read [Gertrude] Stein's marvelous "Melanctha."

•

Notes on Brecht: perfect realism in the acting breathtaking verisimilitude in the dress, gestures, hairstyles, furniture (e.g., in the Hitler Youth scene in *Furcht und Elend*, the mother's hairdo is really a 1935 model, the *Völkischer Beobachter* which the father reads is truly a [copy of the Nazi paper] of that date). But the realism is framed, contained in something larger, just as the actors play on a raised platform on the stage, a smaller stage on the stage itself.


7/13/58

Athens

Every person has his mystery.

The way each man dances to the bouzouki music expresses his mystery. He is praying to himself. He propitiates his own mystery, he is transported, he experiences a catharsis.

The drugged look of the dancer. He plays on the edge of equilibrium. He is a serpent and coils his body. He is a bird and revolves his arms like wings. He is an animal and stoops to all fours.

The dancer slaps his thigh or pinches himself, to keep manageable his state of possession.

While one dances, the rest watch. Each dances alone. The watchers hiss to keep away unfriendly spirits. When he is finished they may toast the dancer's health; they do not applaud, for it is not a performance.

·

The bouzouki singer, a small woman with a big head and short arms and a voice which is part witch, part child— which laments and pleads and exults and whines . . .

·

Tasting a new city is like tasting a new wine.

*[Loose-leaf page, undated except for the notation 1958]*

Illicit are the most perfect loves.

Close connection between paranoia + sensitivity.

[The Marquis de] Sade's "apathy therapeutic."

New York: all sensuality is converted to sexuality.

7/14/58

. . . Living with H means to live through an all-out assault on my personality—my sensibility, my intelligence, everything but my looks which instead of being criticized are resented.

But it is good for me, I think—having nothing to do with the fact that this criticism comes from the person I love. I *have* grown complacent in the years with Philip. I grew accustomed to his flabby adulation, I ceased to be tough with myself, and accepted my defects as loveable since they were loved. But it's true—what H charges—I'm not very sharp about other people, about what they are thinking and feeling, though I'm sure I have it in me to be empathic and intuitive. My senses became dull, particularly the sense of smell. Perhaps it was necessary, this turning inward and deadening of my sensibility, of my acuteness. Otherwise I should not have survived. To remain sane, I became a little stolid. Now I must begin to risk my sanity, to re-open my nerves.

Further, I learned many impoverishing habits from Philip. I have learned to be indecisive. I have learned to speak repetitively, to repeat the same observation or proposal (because he doesn't listen, because nothing is heeded unless said many times, because his agreeing to something once is not treated by him as binding). Philip is extremely unobservant about what other people in his presence are thinking and feeling (remember the [Professor Frank] Manuel interview fiasco at Brandeis 6 years ago), what preoccupies them, etc. *I* have become less feeling, too—despite all the post-mortem sessions in the car after parties and interviews and conferences in which I tried to coach him how to be somewhat aware.

Also P persuaded me of his idea of love—that one can *possess* another person, that I could be an extension of his personality and he of mine, as David would be of us both. Love that incorporates, that devours the other person, that cuts the tendons of the will. Love as immolation of the self.

•

My gestures are languid, e.g., the way I comb my hair, the pace at which I walk—H is right, though not right to resent it.

•

*Remember.* My ignorance is *not* [*underlined twice in the journal*] charming.

Better to know the names of flowers than to confess girlishly that I am ignorant of nature.

Better to have a good sense of direction than to describe how I often get lost.

These confessions amount to boasts, but I have nothing here to boast about.

Better to be knowing than innocent. I am not a girl anymore.

Better to be decisive, willful, than polite, yielding, deferring to the other person's choice.

Admitting my mistakes, when I've been cheated or taken advantage of—a luxury that should be rarely indulged. People may seem to sympathize, really they despise you a little. Weakness is a contagion, strong people rightly shun the weak.

·

P sends me letters filled with hate and despair and self-righteousness. He speaks of my crime, my folly, my stupidity, my self-indulgence. He tells me how David is suffering, weeping, lonely—how I am causing him to suffer.

I shall never forgive him for having tormented David, for having staged this year so that my baby must suffer more than he had to. But I don't feel guilt, I feel sure these wounds to David are not too grave. Baby, sweet boy, forgive me! I shall make it up to you, I shall keep you with me and make you happy—in a right way, without being possessive or fearful or living vicariously in you.

Philip is contemptible. There will be a war to the death between us—over David. I accept that now, I won't give in to pity, for it is his life or mine.

His letters are one howl of pain and self-pity. The basic plea is a threat, the same threat advanced by the old Jewish mother (his mother with Marty [*Philip Rieff's younger brother*]) to the captive son or daughter: Leave me— or, marry that shikseh [*Martin Rieff married a Catholic woman*]—and I'll have a heart attack, or I'll kill myself. P writes: "You are not you. You are us . . ." Then follows a catalogue of his wretched physical state—weeping, insomnia, colitis. "I shall die before I am forty."

Exactly! If I go back to him, I am not I. He could not have put the issue more sharply. Our marriage is a sequence of alternating self-immolations, he in me, I in him, we both in David. Our marriage, marriage, the institution of the family which is "objective, right, natural, inevitable."


7/16/58

Delphi

Fantastic mountains and pinkish cliffs, the sea lying dully in the valley as at the bottom of a huge bowl, smell of pine trees, grey marble columns lying on their sides like logs— half immersed in the ground, cicadas screaming, donkey bells and donkey cries (the counterfeit of agony) which echo against the cliffs, the dark moustached men, hot sun, vibrating silver-green of the olive trees planted in terraces down the hillside, smiling old women—

I think I can live without H after all . . .

7/17/58

Athens

Athens would make a good setting for a story—about for-
eigners, traveling. It has lots of clear-cut and attractive props.

The plump American queens of Athens, the dusty streets
filled with construction work, bouzouki bands in the taverna
gardens at night, eating plates of thick yoghourt and sliced
tomatoes and small green peas and drinking resinated wine,
the huge Cadillac taxis, middle-aged men walking or sitting
in the park fingering their amber beads, the roasted corn
sellers sitting on street corners by their braziers, the Greek
sailors in their tight white pants and wide black sashes,
strawberry sunsets behind the hills of Athens seen from the
Acropolis, old men in the streets sitting by their scales who
offer to weigh you for one drachma—

*[Undated, but certainly written during the trip SS and H. took
to Greece in July 1958]*

No large free emotional gestures left in the repertory of
our marriage—ever narrowing circles of dissatisfaction +
dependence

# 1959

The ugliness of New York. But I do like it here, even like *Commentary* [*magazine, where SS had been taken on as an editor and to which she contributed articles and reviews*]. In NY sensuality completely turns into sexuality—no objects for the senses to respond to, no beautiful river, houses, people. Awful smells of the street, and dirt . . . Nothing except eating, if that, and the frenzy of the bed.

•

Adjusting to the city vs. making the city answer better to the self.

4/3/59

Reading *Crime and Punishment* and Blake's *Milton*. Want to read Apollinaire.

*[The following entry, undated but almost certainly written in the spring of 1959, concerns Elliot Cohen, the first editor of*

Commentary *magazine, where SS worked after coming to New York City that January. Toward the end of his life, and while SS was with the magazine, Cohen began to go mad.]*

Elliot Cohen—

> entire life ruled by passion for manipulation. Saw everything in terms of power. "Elliot had judgment. He knew people. He *liked* to surround himself with people of integrity, to use them." [*Who is being quoted here is unclear, but it was probably Martin Greenberg, a colleague of SS's at* Commentary.]

> "our ailing fisher king"

> wife worked at Mt. Sinai; son, Tom, in a television studio

> 1 W. 85th St. The West Side

> his anti-Communism in the 50's; Communism in the 30's

> born in Mobile, Alabama

> discovered [the critic Lionel] Trilling

> Bob Warshow [writer, *Commentary*'s film critic] talked of him on his hospital deathbed to Martin [Greenberg?], hated him

• 

Exuberance is beauty (Blake)

4/12/59

I am in bad shape. I write it out here; I write slowly and I look at my handwriting which looks OK. Two vodka martinis with Marty Greenberg. My head feels heavy. Smoking is bitter. Tony and a curd-faced bloke ([the social critic] Mike Harrington) are talking about Stanford-Binets. Kleist is wonderful. Nietzsche, Nietzsche

6/12/59

Good orgasm vs. bad.

Orgasms come in all sizes: big, medium, little.

Woman's orgasm is deeper than the man's. "Everybody knows that." [*In quotation marks but unattributed in the journal.*] Some men never have an orgasm; they ejaculate numb.

Fucking vs. being fucked. The deeper experience—more gone—is being fucked. Same for lying on top vs. lying underneath. For years I[rene] couldn't have an orgasm lying underneath, because (?) she couldn't accept the idea of completely letting go, of being "had."

The dike who is "pure masculinity," won't ever let her partner touch her.

*[Undated, but almost certainly early summer 1959]*

Roman army units

> Century—100 men
> Maniple—200 men
> Cohort—600 men
> Legion—6 cohorts (6000 men)

•

"Je suis la plaie et le couteau!
. . . Et la victime et le bourreau."
                    —Baudelaire

"J'ai fait des gestes blancs parmi les solitudes."
                    —Apollinaire

"The idea of the Home—'Home, Sweet Home'—
must be destroyed at the same time as the idea of
the Street."
                    —Piet Mondrian

"Cursed be that mortal inter-indebtedness . . .
I would be free as air: and I'm down in the whole
world's books."
                    —Melville

*[Undated, but also almost certainly early summer 1959]*

results of my stifling my aggression

(A) belief that men have permission, women don't [which leads to] fear of men; dynasty of frail, delicate, weeping women
(B) *can* get angry at physical aggression because my mother is *physically* weak (that's not associated with her—*au contraire!*)

Wearing pants (looking sloppy) equals being a child, not being grown up (+ mannishness)

When a child I have less force—am more vulnerable, more of a victim

*[Undated, but almost certainly fall 1959]*

JEWS  Hebrew: haf (spoon), Mash heh (drink)—noun, yada (know—sexually)—verb, i.e., had intercourse

The anti-Semitic measures of the Lateran Council of 1215

Expulsion from England—1290

Psalmist has "hater" (companion; fellow-worshipper; more than merely friend) in Ps. 119:63

Year is 1519 [*sic*] (1958–59)

  Rosh Ha-Shanah
  Yom Kippur

Hanukkah
Purim
Pesach

Teddy Roosevelt a big philo-Semite; that's why all the German Jews are Republicans

Warsaw Ghetto—April 19, 1943 (Passover)

For the educated Jew in America today, the rejection of Christianity is a pre-requisite to choosing Judaism

Impress of Judaism on my character, my tastes, my intellectual persuasions, the very posture of my personality

The continuing effort to justify being Jewish

Jews emigrated to India from the Iraqi communities of Baghdad, Mosul, + Basra during the 19th C

Malachi inveighs against polygamy

"Histadrut"—Israel General Federation of Labor

Ethiopia has replaced Iraq as one of the main sources of meat supply to Israel

Israel has 5 institutions of university level

1. Hebrew U. at Jerusalem
2. Technion at Haifa
3. Bar-Ilan U. at Bnei Brak
4. Tel Aviv Municipal U.
5. Weizmann Institute of Science at Rehovot

Aliyah = immigration to Israel

The six-pointed star is called the "Magen David"—the shield of King David

Meaning of Ladino in Spanish today!

•

look at—

David I. Grossvogel, *The Self-Conscious Stage in Modern French Drama* (Columbia University Press, 1958) Adamov, Ionesco, Apollinaire, etc.

Novels—

John Barth, *The End of the Road* (Doubleday, 1958)

Stanley Berne, "Bodies + Continents" (in *A First Book of the Neo-Narrative*, 1959)

•

Harold Rosenberg, *The Tradition of the New* (Horizon Press, 1959)

•

Literary Agents (NYC)

J. F. McCrindle

John Shaffner

Toni Strassman (James Purdy)

Candida Donadio (Alfred [*Chester [1928–71]*,
*experimental American fiction writer, author of*
The Exquisite Corpse, *whom SS met through*
*Irene Fornes*])


*[Undated, also fall of 1959]*

World of Françoise Sagan—a group of Parisians, most of
them connected with the arts, who form a circle of unre-
quited sexual infatuation.


*[The following entries are undated, but this notebook was*
*almost certainly filled in the fall of 1959.]*

Mies van der Rohe: "Less is more."

Jane Austen: "I write about love + money. What else is there
to write about?"

Kafka: "From a certain point onward there is no longer any
turning back. This is the point that must be reached."

•


Ionesco's anti-Britishism—makes nonsense of *The Bald*
*Soprano* to play it as an American suburban living room.

•

*New Yorker* [magazine] style:

Upper-middle-class diction laced with colloquialism.
Gives the impression of wry gentlemanliness—of
an intelligent amateur—can't communicate perception or deep feeling

My mother improved her manners by losing her appetite

*[Undated, fall 1959]*

Result of self-consciousness: audience and actor are the
same. I live my life as a spectacle for myself, for my own edi-
fication. I live my life but I don't live *in* it. The hoarding
instinct in human relations . . .

September 1959 [*otherwise undated*]

1. Be consistent.
2. Don't speak about him to others (e.g., tell funny
   things) in his presence. (Don't make him self-
   conscious.)
3. Don't praise him for something I wouldn't
   always accept as good.
4. Don't reprimand him harshly for something he's
   been allowed to do.
5. Daily routine: eating, homework, bath, teeth,
   room, story, bed.
6. Don't allow him to monopolize me when I am
   with other people.
7. Always speak well of his pop. (No faces, sighs,
   impatience, etc.)

8. Do not discourage childish fantasies.
9. Make him aware that there is a grown-up world that's none of his business.
10. Don't assume that what I don't like to do (bath, hairwash) he won't like either.


October 1959 [*otherwise undated*]

I'm not pious, but co-pious


11/19/59

The coming of the orgasm has changed my life. I am liberated, but that's not the way to say it. More important: it has narrowed me, it has closed off possibilities, it has made alternatives clear and sharp. I am no longer unlimited, i.e., nothing.

Sexuality is the paradigm. Before, my sexuality was horizontal, an infinite line capable of being infinitely subdivided. Now it is vertical; it is up and over, or nothing.

•

The orgasm focuses. I lust to write. The coming of the orgasm is not the salvation but, more, the birth of my ego. I cannot write until I find my ego. The only kind of writer [I] could be is the kind who exposes himself . . . To write is to spend oneself, to gamble oneself. But up to now I have not even liked the sound of my own name. To write, I must love my name. The writer is in love with himself . . . and makes his books out of that meeting and that violence.

11/20/59

I have never been as demanding of anyone as I am of I. I am jealous of everyone she sees, I hurt every minute she goes away from me. But not when I leave her, and know she is there. My love wants to incorporate her totally, to eat her. My love is selfish.

Hindu mythology:

4 principle idea[s] // embodied in 4 "persons"

> Creation—Brahma
> Preservation—Vishnu
> Destruction—Siva
> Renovation—Krishna

Shelley, following *John Frank Newton* (Shelley met him [in] 1812) interpreted Plato as [an] Orphic poet presenting the Orphic scheme of salvation in his dialogues (the esoteric Neo-Platonic interp. of Plato)

Shelley has Demogorgon in *Prometheus Unbound* say, "The deep truth is imageless." Poetry is itself a "dome of many-coloured glass" which "Stains the white radiance of Eternity."

Cf. [Thomas Love] Peacock, "Memoirs of Shelley"

Orphic diet (Pythagoras, too): no animal flesh (purifying)

Orphism derived from Hinduism??

Cf. Shelley's comments on Plato's view of poetry in "A Defence of Poetry" (written in answer to Peacock's mocking attack on poetry in "[The] Four Ages of Poetry")

•

Georg Christoph Lichtenberg, *Gedenkbuch*: "As nations improve, so do their gods."

•

Kant: morality = law

•

"jejeune" does not mean "callow"

"transpire" does not mean "occur"

•

"To write is to exist, to be one's self." (De Gourmont)

12/21/59

Tonight she [Irene Fornes] went from work to meet Inez at the San Remo, Ann Morrissett [journalist and playwright] was there. After, the Cedar Bar. She came home at 12:00; I was asleep . . . She came to bed, told me about the conversations of the evening, at 2:00 asked that the light be put out, went to sleep. I was paralyzed, mute, swollen with tears. I smoked, she slept.

12/24/59

Jacob [Taubes's (1923–87)] phone call last night re his conversation with Marcuse last Wednesday.

I have an enemy—Philip.

My desire [*SS first wrote "need," then crossed it out*] to write is connected with my homosexuality. I need the identity as a weapon, to match the weapon that society has against me.

It doesn't justify my homosexuality. But it would give me— I feel—a license.

I am just becoming aware of how guilty I feel being queer. With H, I thought it didn't bother me, but I was lying to myself. I let other people (e.g., Annette [Michelson]) believe that it was H, who was my vice, and that apart from her I wouldn't be queer or at least not mainly so.

I connect my fear and my sense of guilt with Philip, with his publicizing it to everyone all over the world, with the prospect of another custody suit next summer. But perhaps he only makes it worse. Thus, why do I continue the deception with Jacob [Taubes]?

Being queer makes me feel more vulnerable. It increases my wish to hide, to be invisible—which I've always felt anyway.


12/28/59

. . . Til now I have felt that the only persons I could know in depth, or really love, were duplicates or versions of my own wretched self. (My intellectual and sexual feelings have always been incestuous.) Now I know + love someone who is not like me—e.g., not a Jew, not a New York–type intellectual—without any failure of intimacy. I am always conscious of I.['s] foreignness, of the absence of a shared background—and I experience this as a great release.

# 1960

Cogito ergo est

1/3/60

From Gorky's *Reminiscences of Tolstoy, Chekhov, and Andreyev*:

> "Somewhere Nietzsche said, 'All writers are the lackeys of some morality or other.' Strindberg is no lackey. I am a lackey + I serve a mistress whom I don't believe and don't respect. Do I even know her? Perhaps not. So you see what the matter is. It's very sad + depressing as far as I'm concerned, Anton Pavlovich. And since you aren't having a very happy time of it either, I won't discuss my heavy spiritual fetters."

1/11/60

I put a positive layer on top of my negative feelings . . .

. . . Coleridge as an I-Thou philosopher . . .

. . . The octave of her breasts.

Stendhal on social behavior or art (?): "Create an effect, then leave quickly."

I like him. And I wish I could have loved him. (Or: I don't like him. But I wish I could have liked him.) So I make him a present of this feeling.—I mean this as a gift and as a dismissal—But he now believes I do love hm. He tries to cash my bad check and it bounces.

I only meant to be kind. But now I have become a fraud, and I feel imposed on, oppressed by him.

I'm too ashamed to tell him the check is no good and to throw it away. (I was counting on him not trying to cash it!)

He calls for payment. I drop the steel curtain: stop answering the phone or opening letters, cross the street to avoid him.

•

    I: You know why you find it so hard to stay alive?
      You've been running without gasoline.
    S: How? Is honesty the gasoline?
    I: No, honesty is the smell of the gasoline.

•

I.['s] image: I am wearing a nylon skin. It takes much time + effort to keep in repair, and it doesn't fit perfectly either, but I'm afraid to peel it off because I don't think the human skin underneath can take it.

I'm afraid, I say. I'm afraid that lifting the lid will change my life, make me give things up. I don't want to know what I really think, I say, if that means that I would "give up teaching, send David to an orphanage, and Irene to the White Horse." But I. answers, "Really, nothing matters very much." I begin to cry.

"It's better to hurt people than not to be whole."

To trust my skin.

•

Mother's legacy:

A. "Lie to me, I'm weak"—giving us the idea that honesty equaled cruelty. This was the theme (again!) of this last August when Judith was in revolt and in collapse at the same time, + I attacked Judith for being honest to Mother in front of them both, + Mother said, "Exactly."

B. Her inability to inflict pain: to break the bad news, to take the tack out of the foot—things that had to be done. She would call Rosie, + go into another room until it was over.

"going into another room":

> —my going downstairs [*in the house SS shared with Philip Rieff at 29 Chauncy Street in Cambridge, Mass.*]

to David + Rosie's room, lying down, covering my ears, while Philip spoke to the doctor about the results of the rabbit test (summer '54).

—making I. call H (+ going into the front room while she did it) the Saturday evening I came with David to Thompson Street.

No matter what I have said, my life, my actions say that I have not loved the truth, that I have not wanted the truth.

•

Jacob [Taubes]: [Gershom] Scholem's great work is on the Lurianic caballa. He shows it to be a response to the great Spanish catastrophe, a theological wrestling with the idea of Exile, alienation.

There is no such awareness—in theology or literature—of the great event of our time. The six million are not paid for, cannot be understood as leading to, the State of Israel—so Ben-Gurion could play his game of politics.

•

I. says that H's nastiness is not honesty; it's nastiness. Honesty means being honest all the time, not just when you can afford it. H is uninhibited, in the expression of nasty feelings. But she's not honest.

1/13/60

. . . It may take me five years to understand why I don't like to answer the telephone . . .

... So many levels on which I understand the telephone knot
... And contemporary language, with its facile vocabulary of
self-analysis, helps me to continue to live on the surface of
myself. I can say I am shy; or neurotic; or sensitive to the bar-
baric insult to privacy represented by the telephone. (This
was Wolf Spitzer's theory chez Helen Lynd the other night
when I raised the problem in a bottle to their eyes.)—
I exclude as not even worth considering the "psy"-type
insights such as "My mother made me use the telephone
when I was two," "Black telephones are sexual symbols," etc.

•

Read Justin Martyr's dialogue with Rabbi Trypho—2nd century A.D. (Christianity vs. Judaism)

Re-reading *Anna Karenina*

For several centuries B.C. some Greek temples were main-
tained as retreats, where the emotionally disturbed could
recover in a calm + restful atmosphere ("milieu therapy")

1/14/60

I saw beyond Kant today (really yesterday, it's 1:00 a.m.).
Marvellous classes, the last of the term: I feel great tenderness for about a dozen of these kids—

    1. Kant begins at the right point, taking as paradig-
       matic of the moral situation a state of conflict
       or indecision. Specifically, the conflict between
       inclination + the sense of duty.

He is at the center here: Compare Aristotle who
does moral philosophy by giving us a prescription
for the kind of character a good man will have,
and the range of behavior he will exhibit. (Considers ranges of behavior, rather than individual
concrete decisions.)

2. Hence the categorical imperative is useless.

3. To heal, to make whole.

1/21/60

I hardly think except when I'm talking. That's why I talk so
much.

And that's why I don't write.

•

Alfred [Chester] says I'm extraordinarily tactless.—But it's
not that I'm unkind, or need to hurt people. In fact, I find it
very hard to be unkind—to give hurt. (X) Rather, it's that
I'm dumb, insensitive. H said it, Judith said it, now Alfred.
I. doesn't say it because she doesn't know how dumb I am;
she thinks I know what I'm doing, but that I'm cruel.

X: the sense of being bound, coerced by another person. But
you can't free yourself, you want the other person to free you.
Hence the bitchiness of the X-person in a long-term relationship, though in brief it manifests itself in warmth +
agreeableness.

X in the one-night stand, or on the telephone: the inability to say No.

X connected with the sense of shame. X = the compulsion to be what the other person wants.

·

Inspiration presents itself to me in the form of anxiety.

[*Tucked among the blank pages that follow, a shred of paper reading*]: Blake: Life + "a little curtain of flesh on the bed of our desire."

*[Undated, most likely late January 1960]*

Buy

> J. W. Allen, [*A*] *History of Political Thought in the 16th Century* (Methuen, 3rd ed., 1951)

> G. N. Clark, *The Seventeenth Century* (O.U.P., 1931)

> G. M. Trevelyan, *Blenheim: England under Queen Anne* (Longmans, 1931)

> E. M. Tillyard, *The Elizabethan World Picture* (Chatto, 1948)

> W. W. Fowler, *The Religious Experience of the Roman People* (1911)

Denis de Rougemont, *Passion and Society*
[*This book is crossed out in the list, perhaps after having been bought.*]

R. Briffault, *The Mothers*

Calvin, *Institutes* [*of the Christian Religion*] (2 vols.)

A. D. White, [*A*] *History of the Warfare of Science with Theology in Christendom* (2 vols., 1896)

M. Murray, *The Witch-Cult in Western Europe*

B. Malinowski, *Sex and Repression in Savage Society*
Westermarck, *The Origin + Development of Moral Ideas* (2 vols.)

Hobhouse, *Morals in Evolution*

Anders Nygren, *Agape and Eros*

Karl Barth, *Church Dogmatics* (3 vols.)

Max Weber, *Ancient Judaism* (Free Press)
[*This book is crossed out in the list, perhaps after having been bought.*]

M. Lowenthal, *The Jews of Germany* (1936)

Theodor Gaster, *Thespis: Ritual, Myth, + Drama in the Ancient Near East*

Margolis and Marx, *A History of the Jewish People*

Gerth and Mills, *From Max Weber*
[*This book has been crossed out in the list, perhaps after having been bought.*]

Scholem, *Jewish Mysticism* [*also crossed off the list*]

Schweitzer, *The Quest of the Historical Jesus*

[*Undated, most likely late January 1960*]

Americanisms: up-dated, weather-wise, set up

Slang: cracking up, flipping

[*Undated, most likely late January 1960*]

She would like to think that I do not exist. I, she told me yesterday, represent to her Latin, foreign, good taste, sexual experience, uneducated intelligence (—this is not correct, since according to dictionary, education is development of character + mental powers as well as systematic instruction).

Today after I have forced her to partly uncover the ball bearing where lies the power for these things, she pushes me away. I call her + she comes + begins to make love to me. I want it so badly, yet how can I deceive myself that she ever wanted it—I didn't. But Irene explained that she had never wanted [it] more. The proof, the orgasm. Yet didn't Irene know that she didn't give it to me? That I tore it from her? That's how I deceived myself, when I used as proof the fact that she had never given it before. She never gave it before, + she never gave it to me, I took it. Until she decided to prevent me from taking it, at any cost. Was it a coincidence that this decision had to do with the final breakup with H? Was it not when that happened, she was for the first time face to face with me, + then furious with my presence, with my intrusion.

*[Undated, late January 1960]*

prolepsis—anticipation
prolicide—killing of offspring, esp. before or soon
after birth (L[atin] proles—offspring)
prolix—lengthy, wordy, tedious
sedulous—diligent, persevering, assiduous, painstaking
rebellion (unsuccessful) vs. revolution (successful)

•

*Past + Present*, no. 15 (April 1959): Norman Birnbaum, "The Zwinglian Reformation in Zurich"

•

mythic / heroic

•

read Bush, *Science + [English] Poetry*, Wordsworth, [*The*] *Excursion*, Book IV associating the Greek polytheism w[ith] the religion of nature

English 1880 science fiction novel called *Flatland* [by E. A. Abbott] (Dover)

•

Lyons, the capital of the French Resistance during the German occupation

•

Vlaminck as a young man was a professional bicycle racer

•

1919—Sept. issue of *Der Jude* (ed[ited by] Martin Buber): essay by David Baumgardt on Yom Kippur

•

J. P. Stern, *Lichtenberg* (Indiana University Press)

T. W. Adorno, *Aspekte der Hegelschen Philosophie* (Frankfurt am Main, 1957)

For D.: Pantheon ed[ition] of *Grimm's Fairy Tales* (NY, 1944) with intro[duction] by Joseph Campbell

•

*[Readings for the course on the Sociology of Religion SS was to teach in the spring term of 1960 with Jacob Taubes]*

    1) Letters of Paul
    2) Lindsay, etc.: spirit / charisma v. law / institutions
    3) *Christianity and Christendom* (S[øren] K[ierkegaard])
    4) Sohm + Weber

•

1/29/60

The dormitory stink-house of the soul

Important to become *less* interesting. To talk less, repeat more, save thinking for writing.

•

pleasure of tragedy is vicarious suicide

*[Undated, most likely late January 1960]*

Series of stories (à la Strindberg, *Married*)

1   the redemptive marriage
2   sex war
3   second marriage
4   crossing class
5   Don Juanism
6   marriage broken by homosexual affair
7   letter to my husband (from wife who has left)

Notes on Marriage

Marriage + the whole of family life is a discipline, often likened (in Eastern Orthodoxy) to that of monasticism. Both rub away the sharp edginess of personality, as pebbles tossed together by sea waves rub each other smooth in the long run

*[Undated, also most likely late January 1960; after a long aca-
demic discussion of vice and virtue not reproduced here, SS
writes out the following paraphrase of a quote from Nietzsche]*

Don't be kind. Kindness is not a virtue. Bad for people you're
kind to. It's to treat them as inferiors, etc.

•

The elegant malice of Oxford

Theme of Hawthorne: isolation v. communion

Yeats, Brecht, Lorca

Canon, repertoire

Existentialist theme of the search for a true identity

Ramón Sender was (at time of [Spanish] Civil War) editor of
the brilliant liberal Madrid newspaper *El Sol*

•

. . . Silent [film] star face—emphasis was on the eyes; now—
on the mouth

Don't have the same type of close-ups any more—face looking at audience, seducing, entreating, etc. [Now] face looks at
another face on the screen

I.: In painting, I came to understand the value of destruc-
tiveness

•

as many levels of sex as there are of intellect

*[Undated, most likely early February 1960]*

Adventitious [*A box is drawn around the word in the journal.*]

I don't like writers who ignore the queerness that has come into contemporary life since the Bomb.

50's:

> Saul Bellow: *Augie March*—whole-hearted accept-
> ance of American life; figure of the auto-didact who
> comes out of swarming American man

> Ralph Ellison

> Baldwin

> [Herbert] Gold

> Algren

> Malamud

> Coming to terms with the reality of the American
> experience

Last year:

> Thomas Berger, *Crazy in Berlin*—novel

Alfred Grossman, *Acrobat Admits*—the stupefyingly familiar, the fiendishly accurate eye for the minutiae of middle-class Jewish life, parodies on Am[erican] literary or TV styles

Grace Paley, *The Little Disturbances of Man*—stories

Philip Roth, *Goodbye, Columbus*—stories

Metropolitan writers

Jewish

Cranky prose-poetry

50's: Saul Bellow

2/4/60

The Platonic view of Kant is right. I saw this in my Descartes lecture at S[arah] L[awrence College] this morning.

Truth as correspondence to the facts means that the model of truth is conceived of as *information*.

It is true that:

> "It is raining outside."
> "Kabul is the capital of Afghanistan."

+ these statements are true statements because it *is*, Kabul *is* the capital of Afghanistan. Introspection will never get you these results.

But what of:

"2 + 2 = 4."
"It is wrong to make little children suffer."

2/7/60

I. thinks "X" is the reason I can't talk to two people at a time (but always focus on one) and also why I block other people out—even casual intruders like waiters—when I am with someone . . .

. . . What creates "X" is my feeling that each person I am with must be No. 1 with me.

So with each person I betray everyone else. Then after I feel guilty, my accounts are messed up again . . .

. . . Mother was never angry with me, only hurt. (Thank God, I don't do this to David.) I. says the same was true of her mother, though in a less intense form. H's mother was always in a loud hysterical rage—maybe that's why *she* doesn't feel X.

I felt X in Chicago. That's why I wouldn't answer my buzzer in the dorm, + had a code ring which I gave only to Sheldon and E.

I got myself in an X relationship with St. Anne's [College, Oxford].

I didn't feel X toward Philip. Because I was satisfying his demands as well as I could, because I wasn't discussing him with anyone else, because he *was* #1.

*[Undated, most likely mid February 1960]*

"The sane man disappears and is nowhere when he enters into rivalry with the madman."

Phaedrus 245

*[Undated, most likely mid February 1960]*

The churning inside the head—day-long conversations with the absent lover, impulses, fantasies

2/18/60

I. and I don't really talk any more. Already we are weary, aware that everything has been said or at least that more has been said than has been acted on (that our doing is arrears of our talking). The sediment of resentment accumulates, and it seems the civilized thing to avert one's eyes.

I remember when I first became aware of this with P. It was only a couple of months after we were married. The first quarrel was a shock (in the Midway Drexel, about my throwing my dirty sox on the floor of the closet;—and how I wept a week or so later when I read *The Beautiful + the Damned*, how they quarreled) but even worse was when we quarreled but no longer made up. At first we would quarrel, be very upset, silent, non-speaking; then one of us would break the silence to explain, to beg forgiveness, to recriminate further; the quarrel was only over when we flung away the grievance, regretted the incident, wept, made love. But then it started happening that we quarreled, + the quarrels lasted. There was a weary, pained silence of a day or two—or perhaps just

238

a night—and then, imperceptibly, the routines + obligations of the day (of a life lived completely in common, which means buying the groceries + changing the sheets and wondering where your other shoe is) force one to talk, to be amiable, and the thread is picked up, and the quarrel not abolished but covered over, by mutual consent.

This has happened to I. and me. Not because we love each other less (?) but because each feels as more solid, more opaque the limits of the other.

How many times can you complain about the same thing?

•

Reading I.'s recent notes two weeks ago gave me the same bad feeling I had when I used to read H's. It was not that I again found myself being regarded harshly and with disappointment. Rather it was the glimpse of myself reading the notes that disturbed me, perennially looking for my bearings in the opinions of others.

•

(Taubes)

Aristotle vs. Hegel:

Hegel compatible with Christianity, Aristotle not

In Hegel there is the possibility of conversion ("Breaks"); in Aristotle: natural growth, man becoming more human, fulfilling the natural end

Hegel has *time, freedom, history*—none of which
Aristotle has. Hegel is typical of *modern* philosophy

•

read:

Ortega y Gasset, [*On*] *Love* (Meridian)

first part a criticism of Stendhal's book on love
(doctrine of crystallization), egotism, "intellectual
analysis"—obvious that Stendhal never loved

second part: Lady Hamilton. What did this con-
cealed woman have that these great men loved her

2/19/60

(I.)

Two things are meant by "being passive." Being done to. Not
responding. These are entirely different. In the first you can
be "active"(?)

Alfred says he feels cheated by the years of being active sexually. Feels he has deteriorated sexually, his penis is less sensitive. His whole body, too.

Which has more pleasure? The thumb or the mouth? The
mouth. Why?

9:30 [p.m.]

I. walked out an hour ago. From one minute after she left (and I slammed the door behind her) until now I've been puzzling over why I didn't say, "Please don't go" (that she couldn't have agreed to) and then, "Please wait so we can talk" (David being about to go to bed). But I didn't say anything like these things. I just felt enormous anger at her, exactly as you feel toward someone who has just announced that she is about to cause you terrible pain.

I've also been busy excusing myself—I'm still sick, I'm very depressed + somewhat frightened about the discharge, David is sicker + was in the next room, the phone might ring. But that's not important. What's so hard to accept is that I. is fallible, and temperamental, in short (how silly it sounds) not perfect . . . That she is "my poor darling"—as I am to her, as all darlings are.

The reason I rarely succeed [these words replace "can never," which are crossed out] in comforting her when she is depressed, and never succeed in placating her when she is angry with me, is that I always assume she must be right. And being right, she *must* be stronger.

If she is angry with me, all I know ["feel" is crossed out] is that I have done something wrong + she is punishing me. Would anyone try to coax or cajole the person who is meting out the deserved punishment?

Also the idea that she would ever say something she didn't mean—or that I have to interpret what she says, to try to understand it—is so foreign to the way I have always thought of her.

Perhaps that is part of why I was so shocked and pained to read in her notes that she has doubted her love for me, at times, from the beginning.

It's hardly to my credit that I *didn't* doubt it, that I did believe it was a miracle.

I *should* have doubted it. But I was so bent on deciding and acting. I was and am too hasty in proclaiming and in repealing my feelings.

. . . I remember how for the first week I kept asking her (though I didn't really doubt) if she loved me and how she loved me, as if her feeling would from the beginning be the standard both of us would accept.—It has been, in a curious way.

The last time she went—in November—I thought I was having a heart attack. Now I am scribbling. The measure in numbness of the last three months' battle between us.

I told her tonight she is always putting me in the position of saying "I'm sorry."

She told me to go read a sex manual.

So hard to rid myself of the idea that she can't [ *"be angry with me"* is crossed out] feel mistreated by me because *she* is stronger! As if she were making an enormous mistake + treating me as an equal.

•

12:00

I. must be wondering whether to come home now (this home that she never calls home). Maybe she has decided already not to this evening.

So many stalemates between us: this apartment, our home together; sex; David; job.

Why haven't I told I. to give up the apartment downtown? Why hasn't she looked for a bigger place? Why haven't we gone down there + gotten her things? Our talking about that and even going through the motions of resolving to do it reminds me of the way P and I used to talk often about using double contraception + starting to have sex again. It never came close to happening—to our *doing* anything about it, it was just talk. We must have known.

. . . As the present is frustrating, the past is more real. How I. remembers our past, so many details that I have forgotten though I remember a lot. In every couple there is one who is the historian of the relationship: with Philip and me, it was I who remembered; with I. it is she who remembers . . .

*[Undated, February 1960]*

In America, the cult of popularity—wanting to be liked by everyone, including people you don't like

*[Undated, February 1960]*

X, the scourge.

"X" is when you feel yourself an object, not a subject. When you want to please and impress people, either by saying what they want to hear, or by shocking them, or by boasting + name-dropping, or by being very cool.

America a very X-y country. Can limit "X" by rules of class + sex behavior, which America has less clearly defined.

The tendency to be indiscreet—either about oneself or about others (the two often go together, as in me)—is a classic symptom of X. Alfred pointed this out at the White Horse the other night. (This was the first time I. and I had talked about X with anyone). Alfred is like me in this way. Alfred has huge chunks of X!

How many times have I told people that Pearl Kazin was a major girlfriend of Dylan Thomas? That Norman Mailer has orgies? That [F. O.] Matthiessen was queer? All public knowledge, to be sure, but who the hell am I to go advertising other people's sexual habits?

How many times have I reviled myself for that, which is only a little less offensive than my habit of name-dropping (how many times did I talk about Allen Ginsberg last year, while I was on *Commentary*?). And my habit of criticizing people if other people invite it. E.g., criticizing Jacob [Taubes] to Martin Greenberg, to Helen Lynd [*sociologist and social philosopher, 1896–1982*] (more temperately, but because she set the tone), to Morton White years ago, etc.

I have always betrayed people to each other. No wonder I've been so high-minded and scrupulous about how I use the word "friend"!

•

People who have pride [*a box is drawn around the word in SS's entry*] don't awaken the X in us. They don't beg. We can't worry about hurting them. They rule themselves out of our little game from the beginning.

*Pride*, the secret weapon against X. Pride, the X-cide.

. . . Apart from analysis, mockery, etc., how do I really cure myself of X?

I. says analysis is good. Since it was my mind that got me into this hole, I have to dig myself out by way of the mind.

But the real result is a change of feeling. More precisely, a new relation between feelings and the mind.

The *source* of X is: I don't *know* my own feelings.

I don't know what my real feelings are, so I look to other people (the other person) to tell me. Then the other person tells me what he or she would like my feelings to be. This is ok with me, since I don't know what my feelings are anyway, I like being agreeable, etc.

•

I first realized I didn't know my own feelings in disagreements over films, with H, in Paris:

[Andrzej Wajda's] *Kanal* (I liked, she didn't)

[Ingmar Bergman's *Summer with*] *Monika* (I didn't, she did)

[Visconti's *Le*] *Notti bianche*—over the character of
Maria Schell, whom she and Annette [Michelson]
loathed

It wasn't that I waited to hear what others said first. I
answered right off when asked what I thought. But then
when I heard what H + Han (*Kanal*), H and Sam (*Monika*),
H and Annette (*Notti bianche*) thought, I realized they were
right + I was wrong, and I couldn't think of any good reason
to defend my opinion.

.

How does one know one's own feelings?

I don't think I know any of mine now. I'm too busy propping
them up and taking them together.

.

I remember expressing amazement (+ feeling superior)
when H said once in Paris that she didn't know whether or
not she had been in love with someone. I couldn't understand what she was talking about. I said that had never happened to me. Of course not. Since for me being in love is
deciding: I'm in love + sticking with it, I'm always well-
informed.

.

I don't know what my real feelings are. That's why I'm so
interested in moral philosophy, which tells me (or at least
turns me toward) what my feelings ought to be. Why worry
about analyzing the crude ore, I reason, if you know how to
produce the refined metal directly?

. . . Why don't I know what I feel? Am I not listening? Or am I turned off? Doesn't everyone naturally have reactions to *everything*? (P used to enrage me because there were so many things he didn't react to—sit in this chair or that, go to this movie or that, order this or that on the menu.)

. . . Why don't we mind when others react X-ily to us? Don't I in fact despise the prematurely balding young man in the faculty dining room X-ing all over the place? Didn't I despise Jacob [Taubes] for trying to be charming, for saying he might try being queer someday to Alfred and Irene last Thursday evening?

I remember how passionately I admired the way Nahum Glatzer would come to Brandeis faculty parties, say at some point in the evening that he would leave at 10:00, and at exactly 10 would get up + no matter what anyone said would leave. Of course, no one usually said anything—just because he looked like a man who was doing what he wanted to do, who intended to do it, *who wasn't in the least tempted to do otherwise.*

There's the secret. Then no one can tempt you.

I remember how P + I discussed Nahum's way of leaving parties, and how I even told Nahum once at his house how much I admired him for it. He just smiled a little, said nothing.

So beautiful and un-X-y he was with us, though apparently so X-y with the Brandeis administration!

*[Undated, but certainly February 1960. During this period, SS noted down her day in detail. What follows are a few representative entries.]*

Saturday:

> Awake at 7
>
> Museum [of Modern Art] at 10:30
>
> I. arrives at 1:00, coffee + lunch: [the film] *Trouble in Paradise*
>
> 4:30–5:00 coffee with I.; talk; she comes with me in a cab to 118th St. to pick up David
>
> Drop I. at 79th St.—she is going to see Alfred Chester
>
> I feed D + put him to bed. A calls to urge me to come to the party
>
> I read the *Listener*—call Jack, H—leave at 9:30
>
> Cab to 14th Street—I buy tickets for [avant-garde film director] Kenneth Anger film and Pirandello party—I leave—Times Square
>
> Bardot movie—home at 4:00 [a.m.]

Sunday:

> Awake at 7:00—rage
>
> Call A[lfred] at 9:00
>
> Jack picks us up at 9:15

Breakfast at Rumplemayer's

Walk in Central Park

Hotel Pierre with Jack + Ann + 2 friends
(Jack and H)

Cab to Alfred's

Lunch with I. + A, at Bocce place

Matinee off—I. and I go to the Commons

Our talk

We return to Alfred at 6:45

I. calls Ann—we all go down, I., A + David + I
to Frank's Pizza

We pick I. up at 8:00 on Hudson St.—go to films
at Carnegie Hall Playhouse

10:30—cab home, put D to bed—I. wants to eat—
sex—no talk—sleep

Sunday [*a week later*]:

Depression, lassitude

I take Benzedrine at 5:00

Cab to Wash[ington] Sq[uare] at 6:00 to meet A

Dinner at Frank's [Pizza]

Coffee after at Reggio's [Greenwich Village café]

Wednesday:

I am tired

CCNY [College of the City of New York]—the classes are good

I call I. at 11:00, tell her I am coming home at noon

Cab home

I get in bed—we make love—I don't come—she tells me she wonders why she hasn't been unfaithful

She comes back to CCNY at 3:15 (I'm late)

We return by cab, eat at Cuban restaurant—

Associated [Supermarket]

D is waiting

I go to Pearl Kazin's—she isn't there—Pearl comes + I. goes to movie—at Israeli coffee house we meet at 12:30

Sex—I don't come

Tuesday:

Fatigue

David out

I. is up—I weep: she says she has a dinner date with Ann Morrissett [writer and playwright]—she is blank, un-X-y, she starts to run water for a bath— I'm bursting, I whimper to myself, weep, leave, walk to Helen Lynd's car on 72nd St. crying—

Drive to S[arah] L[awrence]

More lecture on truth

I call I. at the studio at 12:00—[appointment with] student (Michael Kellenberg) at 12:45

Taylor lecture at 1:00

I borrow $10 from Peter Reed

2 conferences (2–4) on Sartre, bad faith, X

Cab, train, cab home

Bitterness + hurt again—D arrives one minute after—I call I. to come home—she says she will be right there—I try to sleep, David is on the bed reading—I. rings the bell at 6:30—D + I go down—cash check at Associated—sandwiches

Cab to Marguerita's—A takes David up

Jacob [Taubes's] seminar on Hegel (7:10)

Cab to 100th St.—I. talks to her mother—dirty jokes—guava + cheese

Cab home

David to bed

I change into pants

Cab to skating rink—A not there

Coffee Mill—talk about philosophy + my "lust"

Cab home

I make love to I., she doesn't want to, to me

2/21/60

I said to I. last night that the less sex I had, the less I wanted. (How incredible, what has happened to us.) Is this true. Or isn't it rather that when I have a sexual block, and give up sex, that's what I want to go on doing, at least for a while.

*[Undated, most likely spring 1960]*

. . . I never realized how bad my posture is. It has always been that way; I have never stood erect, except when I was pregnant.

It's not only that my shoulders + back are round, but that my head is thrust forward.

I assumed this posture when trying to swim "naturally." So that my head was too far in the water, and by merely turning my head to the left my mouth was still under water and I could not breathe. In order to breathe, I had to bend my neck back + lift my head up, + this wrecked my arm stroke.

•

Charles Ingle, *The Waters of the End* (Lippincott) novel

•

Blackwell's
Broad Street
Oxford
"Aberdeen's"
13th Street + 4th Ave.   25% off on new books

59th + Madison
"Gandin's"  —Fr[ench] periodicals

•

Read:

Kierkegaard on the concept of irony (this was his
dissertation, 1841)

Gyorgy Kepes, *The New Landscape in Art + Science*
(Chicago, P. Theobald, 1956)

E. Gellner, *Words + Things* (1959) 21/ [*price:
twenty-one shillings*]

D. Krook, *Three Traditions of Moral Thought* (1959)
30/

Guthrie, *Orpheus and Greek Religion: A Study of the
Orphic Movement*

Paul Tillich, *Theology of Culture* (Oxford, 1959)

Gunther Anders, *Kafka* 10/6

[*Crossed out in the journal, perhaps after SS had
bought it*] Hans Jonas, *The Gnostic Religion* (Beacon,
1958)

D'Arcy [Wentworth] Thompson, *On Growth + Form*
(1952)

2/25/60

I. puts her hand on my right breast as we sit in the kitchen talking. (I am telling her about Nahum Glatzer.) I stop my words, smile + tell her it is distracting. X, she says. You feel you have to react. Otherwise, you would go on talking.

My librarian's mentality: the inability to throw anything out, finding all things (esp. in words) "interesting" + worth saving.

   —copying down words (e.g. in French)
   —cutting up the English weeklies
   —pleasure I take in buying and in arranging
      my books


2/28/60

Albee's *Zoo Story* is a painful record of X. The man (Peter) is sitting on the park bench, reading. Jerry comes along + says, I'd like to talk—unless you want to go on reading. Of course he wants to go on reading, but he says, Why no, + puts down his book.

X-situations:

   (a) That I sat at lunch with Aiken, Willis Doney, etc., when I was supposed to pick up Joyce Carr (with P) at 1:00 and drive her to the airport
   (b) My evening in Paris (The "Monocle," etc.) with Allan Bloom
   (c) Letting Henry Popkin kiss me

2/29/60

More thoughts on "X":

> X is why I am a habitual liar. My lies are what I
> think the other person wants to hear.

> I have an X-feeling for Sarah Lawrence [College],
> as I had last year for *Commentary*. Why? Because I
> feel I haven't fulfilled my obligations there. I've
> been unpunctual, unprepared, etc.

> But note: it's true. I am delinquent. I missed last
> Thursday's class. I never prepare for the Tuesday
> lectures. I always come after lunch on Thursday
> when my contract says I must be there at 10:00. It's
> true I get away with it, but my feeling for the place
> becomes sick, infected.

> Maybe people who are X-prone *are* habitually
> irresponsible?

> Isn't the problem that I don't know any of the
> degrees between a total enslavement to a respon-
> sibility and ostrich-like irresponsibility? All or
> nothing, what I've been so proud of in my love life!

> All the things that I despise in myself are X: being a
> moral coward, being a liar, being indiscreet about
> myself + others, being a phony, being passive.

I. says she can't understand how someone signs a contract,
commits himself—e.g., to a job, for a year. I said I can't

understand how anyone ever gets out of doing something, extricates himself.

•

I. says I don't satisfy her on "the first level." (Where food, sex, the intellect are—but not romance.) She said H didn't. Meg did—and it was a weakness on her part not to love someone she couldn't respect.

I. says I am ruled by a family image of myself: being my mother's daughter.

•

X is Sartre's "bad faith"

3/7/60

One must distinguish "the truth" from "the truth about." It is true that 1) it was snowing and 2) Aaron Nolan put milk in the coffee he brought me. But the truth about, e.g., I.'s and my relationship is not an inventory of what has happened, what was said, done. It is an interpretation, an *insight*.

. . . There are degrees of "truth about."

What a delicate instrument language is.

3/8/60

Via Benzedrine, the ever-seeping-down impact of Irene, Dr. Purushottam [*Hindu scholar invited to Columbia to lecture by Jacob Taubes*]

Last week, this morning's lectures on Spinoza's ethics, the long meditation on Kant which began in October, yesterday's idea of the difference between "the truth that" and "the truth about."

3/9/60

Thursday night's dream about the actor Kelty:

> I had seen Jerome Kelty's name in the theatre page of the *World-Telegram* [*New York newspaper of the period*] that afternoon. I have a student at CCNY named Keelty, who tells me his name is pronounced Kelty (I thought of that *in* the dream.)
>
> I. says he was Mr. Guilty.
>
> I am sprawling, even lying down in my chair.
>
> My feet are in the aisle.
>
> After, when the play is over, I find several socks under my seat.

3/12/60

The way to overcome X is to feel (be) active, not passive. I feel anxious when the phone rings—therefore I don't answer or I get someone else to. The way to beat that is not to force myself to answer the phone. It is to make the calls myself.

I. is a bully—tonight's episode with the glass in the kitchen. I felt hate for her.

Last weekend threw a switch, and rage + resentment started flowing. Hard to turn that off. Hence last night when I said in my drugged post-migraine sleep, "I hate your mind." I don't. I hate her.

The passivity of the last three months is broken. But instead there is an area of coldness, + rage in me.

I. drawing, surging now. So as not "to deprive me of my reaction"? No apologies, no justifications. Just "I did it; it's what I wanted to do."

No such thing as a temptation. A temptation is a desire, a lust like any other—but one that we regret afterwards + wish undone (or that we know beforehand we will regret after). So it's no excuse to say, "I didn't mean to do it. I was tempted + I couldn't resist." All one can honestly say is, "I did it. I'm sorry I did it."

Feeling hurt is passive; feeling angry is active.

The source of depression is repressed anger. (I. says her father, a man of great rages, was never depressed.)

3/14/60

This week—since our 48-hour separation—hasn't worked. But I don't feel I have the right to be discouraged, much less to complain to I. I am in her debt; I owe her a year of patience.—That sounds ugly and X-y, but it isn't—as long as I feel strong and loving and want to give.

What hurts most is I.'s ceaseless emotional book-keeping, that she judges our past year together—she was miserable, it was a failure. And that's that.

It came to me last night (dinner, pizza, Frank's, with David + I. + Alfred) that I have lost her. Like a bulletin coming into view in Times Square. I wanted to tell her.—(More happened last weekend than I understand yet, or dare to understand.) I told her this morning. She didn't answer.

She has stopped loving me. She isn't turned toward me, her eyes are blank, she has let go.

I should have trusted my instincts last Sunday, when we returned to Alfred's from The Commons. (She was lying on A's bed, trying to call Ann Morrissett.)

Should I ask her if she wants to separate again? She does want it. But I think she wouldn't want to come back.—She wants to be released. Last Friday I released her. Then Sunday I did my number and brought us together again. But it wasn't as much up to me as I thought then.

3/20/60

I believe in piecemeal morality.

Not buying a German car is a gesture of solidarity, an act of respect, a monument of memory.

In Philip there is no love of the truth. To think is to defend his will, his moral responses. First he has his conclusions, then he thinks up arguments to support his conclusions. Thinking is the will propping itself up—no surprises.

Ben Nelson [historian and sociologist] said that last February: Philip isn't interested in the truth.

Didn't he used to say: I'm interested in meaning not truth.

•

To I., to love someone is to expose him. To me, to love someone is to prop him up, support him even in his lies.

The will. My hypostasizing the will as a separate faculty cuts into my commitment to the truth. To the extent to which I respect my will (when my will + my understanding conflict) I deny my mind.

And they have so often been in conflict. This is the basic posture of my life, my fundamental Kantianism.

No wonder my mind is silent + slow. I don't believe in my mind, really.

The idea of will has often come in to close the gap between what I say (I say what I don't mean—or w/o thinking my feelings through) and what I feel.

Thus, I willed my marriage.

I willed custody of David.

I willed Irene.

Project: to destroy the will.


5/6/60

W[ittgenstein]'s banal remark in the letter to Malcolm continues to reverberate. When *he* says that!

I. points out to me how I allow—encourage?—David to have opinions about everything. (Fish is better in Boston than in San Francisco, the curtains shouldn't be taken down, etc.)

I am sick of having opinions, I am sick of talking.


8/8/60

I must help I. to write. And if I write, too, it will stop this uselessness of just sitting and staring at her and begging her to love me again.

•

It hurts to love. It's like giving yourself to be flayed and knowing that at any moment the other person may just walk off with your skin.

8/14/60

[*In capital letters in the notebook*]: I SHOULDN'T TRY TO MAKE LOVE WHEN I AM TIRED. I SHOULD ALWAYS KNOW WHEN I AM TIRED. BUT I DON'T. I LIE TO MYSELF. I DON'T KNOW MY TRUE FEELINGS.

[*Later, SS added*] (Still?)

12/18/60

(1) [Ibsen's play] *Hedda Gabler*: As I. identifies with the pure female victim ([as in D. W. Griffith's film] *Broken Blossoms*), I've always identified with the Lady Bitch Who Destroys Herself.

The stars I've liked—Bette Davis, Joan Crawford, Katharine Hepburn, Arletty, Ida Lupino, Valerie Hobson—especially as a child.

This woman is above all else a lady. She is tall, dark, proud. She is nervous, restless, frustrated, bored. She has a cruel tongue and she uses men badly.

Hedda [Gabler] is really very passive. She wants to be trapped. She crosses off her possibilities as they vanish. She draws the net in on all sides and then she strangles herself.

She is young, so she waits to be old. She is marriageable, so she waits to find herself married. She is suicidal, so she waits to find herself committing suicide.

Her imperiousness is a masquerade.

(2) Hedda is profoundly conventional. She trembles before the idea of scandal. All her seeming unconventionality—e.g., her smoking, her revolvers—stems from what [she] thinks she, being a *lady* (her father's daughter, etc.) can do.

•

Hedda wants to be given continual reasons (rewards) to live. She cannot supply the reasons herself. For all who cannot supply her with reasons she feels contempt. Contempt is her habitual attitude toward others, but her self-contempt is more severe.

Self-contempt and vanity. Detachment + conventionality.

12/20/60

Read *Epitaph for a Small Winner* [by the Brazilian novelist Machado de Assis], [*Many years later SS would write a fore-word to a republication of the book in English*]; re-read [Conrad's] *Under Western Eyes* + Henry de Montherlant

End novel [*SS is working on her first novel*, The Benefactor, *whose main character is named Hippolyte the "H." in this particular journal entry*] with a letter from H?—To?

# 1961

3/3/61

Jackson Pollock:

"I am interested in expressing, not illustrating my emotions."

"I abandoned my first painting on glass, because I lost contact with the painting."

"I try not to improve myself on the painting, which has a life of its own."

·

Actors Studio
432 W. 44
(white building)
betw. 9 + 10 Ave.
1st floor

·

source of X:

> not really liking the person
> maybe I've never liked anyone

4/13–14/61

migraine:

1. "I'm so good, it hurts."
2. I'm hurt, so comfort me.

follows *enduring* something disappointing or disagreeable without complaint

My repressed feelings leak out—slowly

In the form of resentment

A continual leakage of resentment

Nevertheless, without the full strength of the feeling present at any given moment to back it up, my resentment lacks backbone. It takes the form of *appeal* to the other person to clear things up

Two fundamental needs at war within me:

> need for the approval of others

> fear of others

My reproaches are always a *reaction*, not an action. They are reproaches to the other for reproaching me!

I grant to the others all the liberty I deny myself. To express their feelings, to be what they are (because "they can't help it"). The only things that I allow myself to be angry at are:

betrayal of a relation of confidence

refuse to help me


4/14/61

I'm not a good person.

Say this 20 times a day.

I'm not a good person. Sorry, that's the way it is.

The reproaches don't hurt them.


4/23/61

Better yet.

Say, "Who the hell are you?"


4/23/61

Problem of the emotions is essentially one of drainage.

The emotional life is a complex sewer system.

Have to shit every day or it gets blocked up.

Need 28 years of shitting to overcome 28 years of constipation.

Emotional constipation the source of Reich's "character armor."

Where to begin? Psychoanalysis says: by an inventory of the shit. It dissolves under continued—eventually humorous—gaze.

•

Drainage by means of shouting? telling people off? breaking something? This last is Susan Taubes' favorite fantasy. But it doesn't work if the object is *consciously understood* as symbolic.

My problem as a writer is how to be neither totally outside (as with Frau Anders) or inside with Hippolyte [*both are characters in SS's novel*, The Benefactor].

•

Re: Cassirer, Vol. II [*Ernst Cassirer was a German refugee philosopher and a historian of philosophy. At the time SS is writing, he was a professor at Columbia*]: the perceptual space (assumed in mythic thinking) vs. the metric space of science.

Perceptual space is the space of content—of the fundamental differences of left + right, up + down. Metric space is pure, colorless, even, unaccented, empty.

The modern dislocation of sensibility comes from the fact that we still experience space perceptually but we no longer believe our perception—our experience—is true.

There is no primitive mentality (rc space, time, identity, contagion, etc.) as distinct from the modern (scientific; rational) way of understanding.

The "primitive" way of seeing, experiencing *is* the human way, the natural way.

The scientific way is artificial, a product of abstraction. We never believe it, i.e., experience it.

Only now we are taught / believe that the natural mode of experience + perception is *false*, + the artificial mode [which we never experience] is true. A kind of schizophrenia of sensibility results.

Science as a form of alienation of sensibility.

*[One of the notebooks from 1961 is simply a list of films seen. On no occasion is there a break of more than four days between films seen; most often, SS notes having seen at least one, and not infrequently two or three films per day. What follows is a representative sample of three weeks, from March 25 through April 16.]*

March 25    Museum [of Modern Art]

[Gaumont] *Sept péchés capitaux et l'écriture sainte* (c. 1900)

Ben Wilson, *West of the Law* (c. 1927) [starring] Ben Wilson, Neva Gerber

Lambert Hillyer, *Cradle of Courage* (1920)
Wm. S. Hart "SF Crime"; *Hands Up* [starring]
Raymond Griffith

March 26    Embassy

John Huston, *The Misfits* (1961) screenplay:
Arthur Miller, [starring] Marilyn Monroe (Roslyn),
Clark Gable (Gay), Eli Wallach, Montgomery Clift,
Thelma Ritter

March 27    Minor Latham

Josef von Sternberg, *Morocco* (1930) Marlene
Dietrich, Gary Cooper, Adolphe Menjou

March 29    New Yorker

William Wellman, *Public Enemy* (1931) James
Cagney (Tom Powers), Edward Woods (Matt Doyle),
Jean Harlow (Gwen), Joan Blondell (Mamie),
Donald Cook (Tom's brother), Leslie Fenton
("Nails" Nathan)

Stanley Kubrick, *Paths of Glory* (1957) Kirk
Douglas (Col. Dax), Adolphe Menjou (Gen.—),
George Macready (Gen.—), Ralph Meeker (#1),
Timothy Carey (#2), Wayne Morris (Sgt.),
Emile Meyer (priest)

March 31    New Yorker

Ingmar Bergman, *Smiles of a Summer Night* (1955)
Ulla Jacobssen, Eva Dahlbeck, Gunnar Björnstrand

G. W. Pabst, *The Last Ten Days* (1956)

April 1    Museum [of Modern Art]

Lynn F. Reynolds, *Riders of the Purple Sage* [1926]
Tom Mix (Lassiter), Warner Oland

April 3    New Yorker

René Clair, *The Grand Maneuver* (1956) Michèle
Morgan, Gérard Philipe, Brigitte Bardot

[Warner Brothers] Howard Hawks, *The Big Sleep*
(1946) Bogart, Bacall

April 4    New Yorker

Jacques Becker, *Casque d'or* (1952) Claude Dauphin,
Simone Signoret, Serge Reggiani

Michael Curtiz, *Casablanca* (1942) Ingrid Bergman,
Humphrey Bogart (Rick), Paul Henreid,
Claude Rains, Conrad Veidt (Maj. Strasser),
Sydney Greenstreet, Peter Lorre

April 5    Apollo

[Jean Boyer] *Crazy for Love*, Brigitte Bardot,
Bourvil

Mauro Bolognini, *Wild Love*, Antonella Lualdi,
Franco Interlenghi

April 6    Museum [of Modern Art]

Fridrikh Ermler, *Fragment of an Empire* (1929)
Lyudmila Semyonova, Yakov Gudkin

April 7    New Yorker

Laurence Olivier, *Henry V* (1944) Olivier, Aylmer,
Genn, Asherson, Newton

René Clair, *The Ghost Goes West* (1936) Robert
Donat, Jean Parker, Eugene Pallette

April 10    New Yorker

Mervyn LeRoy, *I Am a Fugitive from a Chain Gang*
(1932) Paul Muni (James Allen), Glenda Farrell,
Edward Ellis, Preston Foster, Helen Vinson,
Noel Francis

[Warner Brothers] John Huston, *The Maltese Falcon*
(194[1]) Humphrey Bogart, Mary Astor, Sydney
Greenstreet, Peter Lorre

April 12    Cinema 16

Michael Blackwood, *Broadway Express* (18 min)

Richard Preston, *Black and White Burlesque* (3 min)

David Myers, *Ask Me, Don't Tell Me* (22 min)

Terence Macartney-Filgate, *End of the Line*
(30 min)—Canada

Ralph Hirshorn, *The End of Summer* (12 min)

April 13    Bleecker St.

G. W. Pabst, *Die Dreigroschenoper* (1931) Rudolf
Forster (Mackie Messer), Carola Neher (Polly), Fritz
Rasp (Mr. Peachum), Valeska Gert (Mrs. Peachum),
Lotte Lenya (Jenny)

, *Pow Wow*

April 14    Archive

*The Griffith Report* (USC)

Preston Sturges, *Unfaithfully Yours* (1948)
Rex Harrison, Linda Darnell, Rudy Vallee

April 15    Columbia Humanist Society

V. Pudovkin, *Storm Over Asia* (*Heir to Genghis Khan*
[1928]), Inkijinov

April 16    Beekman

Michelangelo Antonioni, *L'avventura* (1960)
Monica Vitti (Claudia), Gabriele Ferzetti (Sandro),
Lea Massari (Anna), Dominique Blanchar (Giulia),
James Addams (Corrado), Renzo Ricci (Anna's
father), Esmeralda Ruspoli (Patrizia), Lelio Luttazzi
(Raimondo), Dorothy de Poliolo (Gloria Perkins),
Giovanni Petrucci (Young Prince)

5/1/61

I ask Irene to be detached enough to be doctor, and completely loving and open to me at the same time.

The two demands contradict each other.

•

Hating to be criticized is an inevitable response for one who does not feel he has responsibility for his own acts. Such a person views all his acts as coercions; they don't emanate from himself. Of course, then, all criticism is unfair, unjust.

May 1961 [*otherwise undated*]

The book is a wall. I put myself behind it, out of sight and out of seeing.

The movie is a wall, too. Only I sit with other people before it. And it is not as negotiable culturally as the book—which is a wall, a fortress, that can also be converted into ammunition for fire at others—those on the other side of [the] wall whom I will speak to—later.

•

The life of the city: a life in *rooms*, where one sits, or lies down. Personal distance is ruled by the disposition of furniture. In a living room, there is only one thing to do with another person (besides make love—i.e., go to the bedroom): sit and talk. The life of the living room forces talk upon us, and inhibits the capacity for play and for contemplation.

H concludes: better not to have furniture

6/11/61

Read Gavin Lambert's *The Slide Area* and Faulkner's *Light in August.* Two types of vulgar writing

6/12/61

Apropos [filmmaker Roger] Vadim's *Les Liaisons Dangereuses*: to be absolutely lucid entails, always, being active— being in control, passivity, the sense of being helpless, comes from acting the coward in the face of one's own feelings— hence, fearing the consequences

example: 1951, summer, fearing to go to Amexco for fear I would run into H in the presence of P. I wanted to see her, but I cowered at the thought that P would see how unattractive and mannish (as I remembered) she was!

I had not the courage to love H or to defy Philip. I was afraid of both. "I could only handle one at a time."

(Still true today, hélas + mea culpa)

This cowardice, unknowingness in the face of my own feelings, is why I betray those I love, verbally, to others when I refuse to express my feelings for them

•

Being lucid = being active, not wanting to be "good," i.e., not wanting to be liked by each in turn

•

I'm pourrie [*i.e., "rotten"*], with fears that I won't be "allowed to do whatever I want to do"

Because my wanting isn't strong—it fears risks; it demands approval

I still don't know how to be alone—even sitting in a café for an hour. (I am alone now, feeling strong, waiting for Bobbie in the rue Caumartin. But this sense of wholeness is so rare)

To be able to write I have to be lucid, alone, even though I. is in the same room with me

•

My novels [*sic*] don't exist as ideas in my head. As I learn when I try to make plans, notes for them. They exist only as they are written; I am blank before. Just as one can't run a race in one's head, one must wait for the gun to start

*[Presumably this undated, spring/summer 1961 entry that follows is made up of notations for a novel SS never took further.]*

donnée:

    (1) Hedda Gabler–type woman      (INTERDIT)
    (2) X (a woman)               "le Jour de
                                   relâche"

(3) Debris of past house as      *Liaisons*
       museum             *Dangereuses*
(a) elle se veut être lucide

Japanese lover

     (b) elle se veut être sensuoux [*sic*]

to do Laclos in English


neither

     (a) Laurentian rhapsodic discovery
     (b) Sex (promiscuity) as revolt

*cool*


*[Undated, likely the same period as the previous entry]*

*Burke*

principle of repetitive form: consistent maintaining of a
principle in new guises

•

June 9

Vendôme, Ave de l'Opéra: Jerzy Kawalerowicz, *Mère Jeanne
des Anges* (1961) Cinemathèque: Erich von Stroheim, *Foolish
Wives*

June 10

Hollywood, rue Caumartin: Roger Vadim, *Les Liaisons Dangereuses* (1960) Jeanne Moreau Gérard Philipe Annette Vadim

June 12

Studio L'Étoile, Ave. Wagram: Kenji Mizoguchi, *La Vie de O-Haru, Femme Galante*

*[Another undated entry from the same period]*

*Duarte* Philosopher king of Portugal 11th century?

•

*Targum* = Aramaic translation of the Bible

*Talmud* = encyclopedic work containing the discussions + interpretations of Jewish law as found in the Bible and Mishnah

Purely legal sections are referred to as *halakhah*, the non-legal as *aggadah*

Both the Babylonian and Palestinian Talmuds give info on communal life of Jews 2nd C. BCE to 5th century CE . . .

•

Jorge Luis Borges, *Le Labyrinthe*

•

*[This entry concerns a meeting with two editors, presumably regarding* The Benefactor]

Random House
PL 1-2600
Jason Epstein
Joe Fox
Wed. 3:30
A lavender corsage

•

BUY

Michel Leiris, *L'Age d'Homme* [*This title is crossed out, presumably after SS bought it.*]

George Bataille, *L'érotisme*

Robert Michels, *Sexual Ethics*

Torrance, *Calvin's Doctrine of Man* (Lutterworth)

Harnack, *The Expansion of Christianity* [*in the First Three Centuries*]

Brooks Adams, *The Theory of Social Revolutions*

Jean Wahl, *Défense et élargissement de la philosophie.*

*Le recours aux poètes: Claudel* (Paris, 1959)
292 pp.

*Husserl* (Paris 1959) 2 vols.

*L'ouvrage posthume de Husserl: La Krisis* (Paris,
1959) 17 pp.

•

R. Caillois, *Art poétique* (Paris, 1958) 202 pp. 2nd ed

8/10/61

*[The August entries were written during a trip SS took to
Athens and to the island of Hydra for the month of August
1961. This notebook also contains some sketches—outlines of
characters; plot; a few sustained passages—of what in this notebook is called "Confessions of Hippolyte" and would become
SS's first novel,* The Benefactor.*]*

B.B.'s unhappy complacency

•

Why do I despise myself so in my dreams?

I fear I have never used my body. (My dreams tell me . . .)

8/13/61

David never approaches any adult in a friendly way unless
they speak to him first.

When grown-ups talk to David I often answer for him!!

•

I have never understood asceticism. I have always thought it proceeded from lack of sensuousness, lack of vitality. I've never realized that there is a form of asceticism—consisting in simplifying one's needs *and* seeking to take a more active role in satisfying them—which is precisely a more developed kind of sensuousness. The only kind of sensuousness I have understood entails love of luxury + comfort

•

To write you have to allow yourself to be the person you don't want to be (of all the people you are)

Role of scientists vis-à-vis American economy (dependent on preparing for war) is like couturiers in world of clothing—to create standards of obsolescence, so that last years' [*sic*] can be scrapped

•

Writing is a beautiful act. It is making something that will give pleasure to others later

8/16/61

*[In the context of the journal, these two sentences most likely refer to Irene Fornes, but do not do so explicitly.]*

Vulgar, like my mother. In love with power, money success, fame.

·

When something is wrong or doesn't work, it rarely occurs to me to try to repair it. I usually—without thinking—work out a way of seeing the thing without bringing into play the defective part.

Irene is just the opposite, e.g., her reaction to the typewriter (with its bent "?" [key] and ribbon that unwound in only one direction) which I've been using all week and she began to use only yesterday. After typing one line, she set out to fix the machine—and did. She fixed the spool with a piece of paper, found the thing that makes it double space—All this I'd been doing manually—

·

I make contact with people by exchanging cards. Where are you from? Oh, do you know so-and-so? (a faggot if the person is a faggot, a writer if the person is a writer, a professor if the person I'm speaking to is a professor, etc., etc.). Later comes: Have you read—? Have you seen—?

8/23/61

I. said this was the first good orgasm she's had for months, and then I spoiled it.

She is drifting away, fed up, beyond patience with me.

Remember what she proposed the other day, that she take a room when we get back to New York, that we see each other "often."

When you have a tumor, you need surgery, she said. I wept. She took my hand. But she will propose it again, soon.

I said to her today, "I love you," and she answered, "What's that got to do with it?"

I spent an hour this evening (when she was down at the port) masturbating + studying my cunt with a mirror. I told her when she came back. "Did you discover anything?" she said. "No," I answered.

•

FORETHOUGHT

Don't be careless when there is something good. Don't be so sure that whatever follows must be good.

•

When you stop reading and put down the book, you mark the page so you can continue at exactly the same point when you pick the book up again another time. Similarly, when you are making love and stop for a moment (to pee, to take off your clothes) you must notice exactly where you were so that you can resume at that exact point a moment later. And then you must watch very carefully to see if it works, because sometimes—after even the slightest break—it is necessary to begin all over again at the beginning.

•

I.: Sex is hypnosis. Maintaining a rhythm monotonously. (Though not all rhythms are sexual rhythms.) Rhythms in several successive gears.

•

The past is no less a dream.

•

image: a symphony orchestra w/o a conductor, a firm w/o a director, a dream w/o the father

8/24/61

Never to talk about:

1. Philip
2. My childhood, schools, etc.
3. Mother

To Irene.

(Save these for the analyst-cloaca, + don't talk about her [*Diana Kemeny, the analyst SS had begun to see the previous spring*] either)

•

I. said the other day: "With me, sex has been a religion."

•

No place in sex for politeness. Politeness (not delicacy) is uni-sexual.

*[Dated only as "August"]*

[Stendhal's early novel] *Armance*—more discursive, yet swifter; less visual, less dramatic than later 19th-c. novels

N.B. Mme de Malvert's idea that naming Armance's TB will hasten its advance (Ch. 1)—like "words ignite feelings"—as in [Stendhal's] *La Chartreuse de Parme* (Sanseverino in carriage)

•

short story.

Two persons of the same sex and name

The one tormented by envy (> and contempt) for the other

The mirroring of two lives: child, fellowship, divorce, job, resigning job, analyst

9/12/61

*[Next to the date is the notation: Train Praha–Paris]*

1. No *general* statements about my own character, tastes, standards—such as "I never . . ." or "I wouldn't . . ."

   What is deposited in me from my childhood—as standards, rather than inclinations or tastes—I formulate in this way.

E.g., "I wouldn't take David to a clinic" or "I *never* lent H money"—

Tastes, traits don't generalize about themselves; they always assert themselves in the particular instance. They don't become indignant when they aren't anticipated.

Indignation is a good clue that something is wrong—

You wouldn't say, "I *never* drink milk in my coffee!"

The indignation, the general statement, must testify to all the *effort* that has gone into maintaining the attitude. Not that it's *always* against one's inclinations (it probably is in most cases), but at least it's an attitude that hasn't been absorbed, that one "bears," as a duty, an obligation, a rule. And you become indignant when you learn that not everyone acknowledges this duty, + your effort seems of less value because not everyone has made it.

2. About money: [*there is no further entry*]

3. Keeping clean—the problem is connected with sex. I feel "ready for sex" after a bath, but there isn't any; so I'm reluctant to bathe—I fear the awareness of my own flesh that it always gives me. (A memory: the shower—what I said to Danny going to a party on the Near North Side [of Chicago] with her—being asked to leave.)

•

The Parable of the Fatal Disease:

Three weeks ago it would have been cured by two aspirins; two weeks ago penicillin would have been enough; last week an oxygen tent; this week an amputation; next week the patient will be dead. Foolish the doctor who offered penicillin last week! Did he not only fail to cure but even hasten the progress of the disease?

9/14–9/15/61

1. Not to repeat myself

2. Not to try to be amusing

3. To smile less, talk less. Conversely, and most important, to mean it when I smile, and to believe what I say + say only what I believe

4. To sew on my buttons (+ button my lip)

5. To try to repair things which don't work

6. To take a bath every day, and wash my hair every ten days. Same for D.

7. To think about why I bite my nails in the movies

8. Not to make fun of people, be catty, criticize other people's looks, etc. (all this is vulgar and vain)

9. To be more economical (because the carefree way I spend money makes me more dependent on earning this much money)

*[Undated in the notebook]*

I. is right. I must give everything up, or I will always have bile instead of blood, skin instead of flesh.

It doesn't matter. Think of death. Don't try to "appear." I am so self-indulgent: I know nothing of the will.

Think: "It doesn't matter."

Think of Blake. He didn't smile for others.

I don't possess myself. I musn't try to possess anyone else; it's hopeless, for I'm too clumsy.

Don't smile so much, sit up straight, bathe every day, and above all Don't Say It, all those sentences that come ready-to-say on the tickertape at the back of my tongue.

"Do not long," etc.

I must [go] *farther* even than this, which has thus far been too difficult for me.

Beware of anything that you hear yourself saying often.

E.g., the French girl on the train:

> She: "And my sister over there"—(pointing to sister, round adolescent face, sleeping in ungainly position)
> I: "Oh, is that your sister?"
> She: "Yes. We don't resemble each other at all, do we?"

Think how many thousands of times she must have said that, and what feelings lie behind those words—hardened, strengthened, confirmed each time she says them.

*[Further 9/15/61 entry far ahead in the notebook, also marked "en avion"]*

The thought of death, and of measuring my preoccupations against the idea that I might die today.

All projects are mocked.

"Wait . . . I didn't finish . . ."

Sex is not a project (unlike writing a book, making a career, raising a child). Sex consumes itself each day. There are no promises, no goals, nothing postponed. It is not an accumulation.

Sex is the only good of which death cannot cheat us, once we have begun to live sexually. To die after a year of sexual happiness is no sadder than to die after thirty years of it.

Only acts which are repeated, then, are free of the bitter taste of death.

*[Undated, possibly inserted into this notebook six years later (it is impossible to tell whether the date says "1961" or "1967").]*

Some years ago I realized that reading made me sick, that I was like an alcoholic who nevertheless experiences a bad hangover after each binge. After an hour or two browsing in a bookstore, I felt numb, restless, depressed. But I didn't know why. And I couldn't keep away from the stuff.

—Also, the need to sleep after a bout of reading (esp. if I'd been reading several books) reflects this (I used to turn it around—w/o understanding what I felt—and read in this greedy way with several books beside the bed at night, *in order to* fall asleep).

The reason most things look better once bought and out of the store—even on the bus ride home—is that they have already begun to be loved.

(the plastic, etc., doll the French girl was carrying on her purse on the train)

"I like people who exteriorize their feelings."

ouverte, aimable, spontanée

English lack warmth not in the sense of good will but in the sense of the flesh.

*[Undated]*

Camus:

Each time that one (that I) surrender to one's vanities, each time that one thinks and lives for the sake of "appearing," one betrays . . . It is not necessary to deliver oneself to others, but only to those whom one loves. For then it is no longer delivering oneself in order to appear, but only in order to give. There is much more force in a man who appears only when he must. To go to the end, that means to know how to guard one's secret. I have suffered from being alone, but in order to have kept my secret, I conquered the suffering of being alone. And today, I know no greater glory than to live alone and unknown.

To write, my profound joy!

To consent to the world and to enjoy it—but only in nudity.

•

Henry Bellamann Foundation = [prize given] annually
Edith M. Sansom
Director
1534 Conery St.
New Orleans

Huntington Hartford Foundation
200 Rustic Canyon Rd.
Pacific Palisades
Calif.

Fellowship for creative writing

Eugene F. Saxton Memorial Trust
$2500 No fixed date
c/o Harper & Bros
49 E. 33

James Merrill Foundation

•

buy (La Hune) [bookstore in Paris]

Michel Leiris, [*La*] *Possession et ses aspects théâ-
traux chez les Éthiopiens de Gondar* 1958

*L'Homme*, Cahiers d'Ethnologie, de Géographie et
de Linguistique—nouvelle série—No. 1 publiés par
l'École Pratique des Hautes Études (6ème section) et
le Centre National de la Recherche Scientifique
(Lévi-Strauss, etc.)

Librairie Plon
8, rue Garancière
Paris 6e

A. Schaeffner, "Le Pré-Théâtre," *Polyphonie*
(Paris I, 1947–48) pp. 7–14

H. Jeanmaire, *Dionysos, histoire du culte de Bacchus*
(Paris: Payot, 1951)

•

False gentility: "feeling badly"

Shifting in mid-sentence from the dressy "one" to the more
comfortable "he"

•

9/19/61

Something strange is happening to me. I tried to read a book catalogue yesterday + couldn't, + threw it out.—I'm beginning to be able to tell good from bad!

That there are mysteries (not only uncertainties): that's what the Puritan spirit doesn't understand.

E.g., Genet's Saint Divine.

Wanting to sleep in my clothes is connected with not having washed. That's when I want to do it.

Getting thin: a change of identity.

We celebrate our changes of character by altering our personal appearance.

Why doesn't H do this?

Why one can't be an orthodox believer in Christianity, etc., one can't believe that any one religion is *the* vehicle of truth. It is, literally, to deny the humanity of other civilizations. [*This is followed by the following unfinished sentence, which is crossed out.*] Once you transcend the boundaries of your civilization, you

*[Undated in the notebook]*

send for

> *Studies on the Left* Cuba, etc.
> Vol. I, No. 3
> 85 ¢
> P.O. Box 2121
> Madison 5, Wisc

> Librairie Bonaparte
> Theatre, films

> *Antonin Artaud et le théâtre de notre temps* Cahiers
> de la Compagnie Renaud-Barrault

> Kenneth Anger, *Hollywood Babylon*

· 

Pourquoi aurais-je túe cette femme?

Why would I have killed that woman?

· 

M[other]

> "I've reached the stage when . . ."
> "Over the years I've become . . ."
> "Let's face facts . . ."

> Visconti, Ford
> Théâtre de Paris
> 15, rue Blanche 8:30

Goya exhibition
Galerie Gavea
45, rue de la Boétie
Paris VIII
10h–12:30
2h–7h

12/3/61

Becoming aware of the "dead places" of feeling—Talking
without feeling anything. (This is very different from my old
self-revulsion at talking without knowing anything.)

•

The writer must be four people:

1) The nut, the obsédé
2) The moron
3) The stylist
4) The critic

1 supplies the material; 2 lets it come out; 3 is taste; 4 is
intelligence.

A great writer has all 4—but you can still be a good writer
with only 1 and 2; they're most important.

12/9/61

The fear of becoming old is born of the recognition that one
is not living now the life that one wishes. It is equivalent to a
sense of abusing the present.

# 1962

*[The following two entries are undated, but most likely were written in January or February 1962]*

[Novelist and critic] Mary McCarthy's grin—grey hair—low-fashion red + blue print suit. Clubwoman gossip. She is [her novel] *The Group*. She's nice to her husband.

•

I write to define myself—an act of self-creation—part of [the] process of becoming—In a dialogue with myself, with writers I admire living and dead, with ideal readers . . .

Because it gives me pleasure (an "activity").

I'm not sure what purpose my work serves.

Personal salvation—Rilke's *Letters to a Young Poet*

1/7/62

The "cost problem" for the Jews—

Survival as the ultimate value, merit identified with suffering as the means

*Christians take from the Jews* (cf. [St.] Paul) *the whole idea of the value of suffering* (But *not* the goal of survival!) *But the difference is that the Christians have never really lived it, believed it*—except the early martyrs and a few monastics. Nothing in their experience corresponds to it (while the Jew has persecution, pogroms, anti-Semitism, etc.). The Jews not say it but live it.

It's as if a child would be born of aristocratic parents, who were cousins, and the parents of these parents were cousins, + so on back for 40 generations, + this child has leukemia + six fingers on each hand, + syphilis. And someone says to him, "I think you're like that because your parents were cousins," + he says to someone else, "He's just envious because I'm an aristocrat."

Spirit = lucidity / tranquility.

Jews mainly speak of their "rights" (rather than what they want).


Week of Feb. 12, 1962

1. FORMALITY ("please," "thank you," "excuse me," etc.)

Way of not giving yourself to the other person

David has so much of this already, my ceremonious-timid style of being with people

 B. I say "excuse me" when I make an awkward
  movement in sex
 C. I say "you've insulted me" when I'm hurt,
  rejected, etc.

Mother's idea of the Chinese family—

"RESPECT" was what she always complained of not having—from Dad, me, Judith—not that we hurt her, didn't love her. We "offended" her

an instrument of my general tendency to be *evasive*, indirect, not to declare my wishes

I once said to I.: "I'd rather be polite than fair."

2. PREMATURE PLIABILITY agreeableness

So that the underlying stubbornness is never touched

Accounts for 80% of my notorious flirtatiousness, seductiveness

I'm very proud—have as much difficulty expressing sense of humiliation as I used to with anger > all I can do is go to sleep

Cf. trial Feb. 14 [*when PR's court case to gain custody of DSR was heard in a Manhattan court. In fact, PR's visitation rights were cut back. The "Lester" referred to in this entry is Lester Migdal, SS's attorney.*]

I don't admit that I feel humiliated vis-à-vis Lester, upset that he must dislike me, was cold to me on the phone—

I defend myself by prematurely abasing myself. Outdoing the rejection of the other by rejecting (despising) myself first + more. In that way I rob the reaction of its power

3. spoiling what is good (natural, unselfconscious) by talk

    A. e.g., by praising D[avid] whenever (it's so rare!)
       he is charming, when he laughs, his remembering
       the words of songs
    B. e.g., explaining a situation *while* he is experiencing
       it—stuffing his mind with facts

Sunday while Ernst was making a paper swan I told him [*David*] it was Japanese, called origami . . .

4. NEVER ASKING FOR ACCOUNTS

e.g., money—my idea (from M[other]) that it's vulgar

the money comes from "somewhere"

I don't earn it, merit it. There can be no just payment (so more *or* less would be unfair) so any payment is as good as any other

·

About the things I learn about myself:

    1) *I don't generalize*—I go inch by inch—I don't
       tamper with the underlying value which produces

several diff[erent] types of behavior. Each thing
I. says is a separate revelation

2) I must separate *values* from *attitudes*

The neurotic adjustment produces / gets hooked to a value,
an ideal on which it nourishes, sustains itself

e.g., "so good that it hurts" > the Superior Suffering Jew

I still *value* my mother (Joan Crawford, a lady, etc.) even
though I see how wrong, inadequate she is

As I lose my neuroses, I'll lose a lot of my attractiveness?

What I admire / identify with in Monica Vitti ([the star of
Antonioni's film] *L'avventura*) is the opposite of what I
admire in Julien Sorel [the hero of Stendhal's novel *The Red
and the Black*]

•

Experiments + Exercises

1. chewing

2. feeling textures, objects

3. checking shoulders (lowering them)

4. uncrossing my legs

5. deeper breathing

6. don't touch my face so much

7. bathe *every* day (already big progress here in
   last 6 mos.)

8. watch Tuesday night arrogance—irritability—depression. It's Jacob [Taubes]. [He's] P[hilip]'s replacement + the seminar. Teaching for me is intellectual masturbation

3/3/62

The number my mother taught me:

—formality ("please," "thank you," "excuse me," "sorry," "may I")
—any division of attention is disloyalty
—"the Chinese family"

I wasn't my mother's child—I was her subject (subject, companion, friend, consort. I sacrificed my childhood—my honesty—to please her). My habit of "holding back"—which makes all my activities and identities seem somewhat unreal to me—is loyalty to my mother. My intellectualism reinforces this—is an instrument for the detachment from my own feelings which I practice in the service of my mother.

I thought the root was fear—fear of growing up, as if I would, by growing up, relinquish my only claim to not being left, not being taken care of.

I thought this was why I can't give myself steadily (or at all) to sex, work, being a mother, etc. For if I did I would be naming myself an adult.

But I wasn't ever really a child!

The reason I'm not good in bed (haven't "caught on" sexually) is that *I don't see myself* as someone who can satisfy another person sexually.—I don't see myself as free.

I see myself as "someone who tries." I try to please, but of course I never succeed.

I invite my own unhappiness because it's evidence for the other that I'm trying. Behind "I'm so good that it hurts" lies: "I'm trying to be good. Don't you see how hard it is. Be patient with me."

From this, a will to failure that often—except in sex—my talents frustrate. So then I devalue my successes (fellowships, the novel, jobs). These become unreal to me. I feel I am masquerading, pretending.

•

My vaunted infrequency of falling in love and making close friends means, "See, I haven't betrayed you often. Only when the feeling was overwhelming. But not for any casual feelings, one that I wouldn't stake my life."

My compulsive monogamy is:

1) a duplication of my relation to my mother—
   I can't betray or you'll leave me.

Fear

2) You wouldn't be important to me if I were
   unfaithful to you.

Will

Pride [to] stubbornness [to] fear

3/5/62

I subordinate sex to sentiment—in the very act of making love.

I fear the impersonalness of sex: I want to be talked to, held, etc.

The trauma of H.

#1: sex as toughness, meanness. It made me afraid.

American idea of sex as hard breathing (passion). They're indicating, not doing. They think less breathing = less passion, coldness. (I.)

Short cut: don't call sex sex. Call it an investigation (not an experience, not a demonstration of love) into the body of the other person. Each time one learns one new thing.

Most Americans start making love as if they were jumping out of a window with their eyes closed.

Sex as a cognitive act would be, practically, a helpful attitude for me to have, to keep my eyes open, my head up—cf. I.'s fantasy of conducting, or more often, submitting to a medical examination—where the point is *not* to show sexual excitement as long as you can. (No pelvic spasms, no hard breathing, no words, etc.)

I have to make sex cognitive + cognition sensuous—to correct the imbalance now.

Susan Taubes: sex is sacred. The rationalization of willed ignorance. (Don't profane the mystery by looking.)

9/3/62

I am sitting on the grass by the river. David is playing ball with a Puerto Rican boy and man.

Alone, alone, alone. A ventriloquist's dummy without a ventriloquist. I have brain-fatigue and heart-ache. Where is peace, the center?

There are seven different grasses where I am lying

[*Drawing of grasses*]

dandelions, squirrels, little yellow flowers, dogshit.

—I want to be able to be alone, to find it nourishing—not just a waiting.

Hippolyte says, Blessed is the mind with something to occupy it other than its own dissatisfactions.

I dreamed of Nat[han] Glazer [*at the time, Glazer was a colleague at* Commentary Magazine] last night. He came to borrow a black dress of mine, a very beautiful dress, for his girl-friend to wear at a party. I tried to help him find it. He lay on a simple bed + I sat beside him and stroked his face. His skin was white except for patches of black moss-like

beard on his face. I asked him how his face got so white, +
told him he should get into the sun. I wanted him to love me
but he didn't.

Ann oppresses me, Joan doesn't.

I am waiting for David to grow up the way I waited to get
through school and grow up. Only it's my life that will pass!
The three sentences I've served: my childhood, my marriage,
my child's childhood.

I must change my life so that I can live it, not wait for it.
Maybe I should give David up.


9/7/62

*[This entry comes later in the notebook than the one dated
9/15/62]*

All Freud's heroes are heroes of repression (Moses, Dostoyevsky, Leonardo); that's what being heroic is for him.
Work is fun. The ego versus the slob body. That's why he
appealed to Philip. People always ask me (Ann did just this
week) how a man interested in Freud could behave as Philip
does. I guess nobody has read Freud. Sure, he was brilliant
about motives—which Prof. Rieff certainly isn't—but he
(Freud) was a tremendous champion of the self-mutilating
"heroic" will. The psychoanalysis he created [is] a science of
condescension toward the body, the instincts, the natural
life—at best.

9/12/62

Premature pliability, agreeableness, so that the underlying stubbornness is never touched, accounts for 80% of my notorious flirtatiousness, seductiveness

9/15/62 1:15 am

I am sure that I. is in bed with someone this moment. I feel my guts being scalded.

My anxiety last night that I was coming down with pneumonia. The Mexican restaurant + Mexico. I. said in that mad pretentious letter of yesterday: "I can't breathe."

Tearing up the yellow dress.

•

Female sexuality: two types, the responder + the initiator. All sex is both active (having the dynamo inside oneself) + passive (surrendering).

Fear of what people will think—not the natural temperament—makes most women dependent on being desired before they can desire.

Love as incorporation, being incorporated. I must resist that. Should be tension in the palm of one's hand, as the dancing instructor says. You don't get any messages if you're limp.

Try to think of this separation [from Irene] as such a tension. So I can get and give—messages . . . To cut out of the "Despair—I've been rejected" or "Fuck her" alternatives.

In this society, one must choose what "feeds" [*the words
"goes into" are crossed out*]—the body must deprive the
mind, + vice versa. Unless one is very lucky or smart, to
begin with, which I was not. Where do I want my vitality
to go? To books or to sex, to ambition or to love, to anxiety or
to sensuality? Can't have both. Don't even think of the outside chance that I will have it all back at the end.

Something vulgar, nasty, craven, anti-life, snobbish in the
sensibilities of Henry James + Proust. Glamor of money,
dirtiness of sex.

One is either an outside (Homer, Tolstoy) or an inside
(Kafka) writer. The world or madness. Homer + Tolstoy like
figurative painting—try to represent a world with sublime
charity, beyond judgment. Or—uncork one's madness. The
first is far greater. I will only be the second kind of writer.

9/20/62

The mind is a whore.

My reading is hoarding, accumulating, storing up for the
future, filling the hole of the present. Sex and eating are
entirely different motions—pleasures for themselves, for the
present—not serving the past + the future. I ask nothing,
not even memory, of them.

Memory is the test. What one wants to remember—while
still in the act or experience—is corrupt.

Writing is another motion, exempt from these strictures.
Discharging. Paying off the debt to memory.

Sex fantasies of losing autonomy:

slave
medical examination
whore
rape

*[Undated, fall 1962]*

. . . Haunted by the ghosts of those unborn babes whose rudiments were hopefully elaborated in her womb, month after month, only to be blotted up in sterile pads + unceremoniously flushed down the toilet.

*[Undated, fall 1962]*

Books

Origen, *Contra Celsum*

Pritchard, *ANET* [*Ancient Near Eastern Texts*]

~~Morgan, *The Hindu Way*~~

~~Huizinga, *The Waning of the Middle Ages*~~

~~Northrop Frye, *Anatomy of Criticism*~~

Cornford, *The Unwritten Philosophy*

Jane Harrison, *Themis*

George Thomson, *Studies in Ancient Greek Society*
([*presumably bought at*] W. 13th St. Communist
bookstore)

G. Le Bras: *Études de sociologie* [*religieuse*] (Paris:
PUF)

Murray, [*The*] *Political Consequences of the
Reformation*

Gibbon, [*The History of the*] *Decline and Fall*
[*of the Roman Empire*]

Tillich, *The Interp*[*retation*] *of History*

10/16/62

*[Loose-leaf page found among SS's papers]*

Sentimentality. The inertia of the emotions. They are not
light buoyant.—I am sentimental. I cling to my emotional
states. Or do they cling to me?

I wish I could think I. simply takes me for granted. The mas-
sive refusal of intimacy in her letters, the occasional touches
of condescending affection.

Not once "I miss you," not once a word from inside.

But I cannot explain it except by the utter collapse, the pain-
less dissolution of any feeling for me. All the lines are down.

Tiemmi, tiemmi. [*From Dante's* Purgatorio, *Canto XXXI*:
"*Poi, quando il cor virtù di fuor rendemmi, / la donna ch'io
avea trovata sola / sopra me vidi, e dicea: 'Tiemmi, tiemmi!'* "
*("Hold me, hold me.")*]

I thought I. had the key, and only she. That all my sexuality
was bound to her. Now I know that, technically, that's not so.
But, still, I don't believe in the reality of anyone else.

I do not believe she will come back to me. Those who go
away never come back.

—How I lie in my letters to her! I want her to believe I am
tranquil and hopeful—my final magic spell to bring her back.

# 1963

3/26/63

Love the *truth* above wanting to be *good*.

Ask: Does this person bring out something good in me? Not: Is this person beautiful, good, valuable?

*[Dated only April 1963, Puerto Rico, and consisting of ten sheets of paper torn out of a notebook and clipped together]*

The look is a weapon. I'm afraid (ashamed?) to use my weapons.

"Women novelists lack executive force" ([Columbia University English professor] Steven Marcus the other night)—a different relation to their own ego. Prevail through sensibility.

I hate to be alone because when alone I feel about ten years old. (Timid, uncertain, ill-at-ease, plagued by doubts as to whether I have permission to do this or that.) When I'm with another person, I borrow adult status + self-confidence from the other.

Here in the hotel:—how to ask the time over the phone this morning; whether I could take the bathroom towels to the beach; whether I can cash a personal check, etc.

Two dreams last night

—a man (my husband—mad?) trying to kill himself— opening the pipes—flooding the house (concrete blocks)—I escape with the child to the hill above— he follows, tricks me, takes the child down where they both die.

—a student denounces me (about [blank], etc.) in class. (Mr. Mall Wall?) I can't understand why he hates me so. No one in the class supports me. It starts when he is playing the harmonica (very beautifully)—I begin talking, tell him to stop, but he doesn't. I get angry + go + take it away from him. Return to front of the class. He takes out another harmonica. I tell him I will fail him. Then he speaks.

In the other class (C[olumbia] C[ollege]) there is a riot, too. I'm saying something mildly critical about America—suddenly all the students take out small square sheets of paper + set fire to them. (It's a small auditorium.) There is perfect silence. I stop. Then I realize it's a declaration, a signal, a hex. They're all (four-fifths, I say later) members of a student fascist organization. I'm condemned.

Rest of the dream spent waiting in offices to see a dean, to explain. I find Friess. Then he turns into an old woman—he's (she's) busy, has to go home, but accompanies me, while I wait. I explain how sur-

prised I am. In all the years I've been teaching nothing like this has ever happened—then two on the
same day. I decide I will admit to —— when I was
16, but nothing more.

•

I can't understand why I made this trip, except in the hope
that there is a good in being so unhappy—as if I might use
up my large portion of unhappiness, + have only joy left.
I've been miserable every moment in a grim, bewildered
way, with nothing to dilute it or distract myself from it. Like
an illness. I wish all the time I had brought David.

One of the things that is so terrible between I. + me is the
never-ending verbal settling of accounts. Every conversation
is a fresh wound—justification + counter-justification, explanation and counter-explanation. Like the business of my
taste in movies—a fresh wound, a fresh grievance.

Motto of Soichiro Honda, head of world-famous Honda
Motorcycle Company: "Speed is man's right."

My dream of madness: being no longer capable of the effort
to make contact. Absolved of it, by madness.

Stunned + sleepy ever since I'm here—over 24 hours. The
"real me," the lifeless one. The one I flee, partly, in being
with other people. The slug. The one that sleeps and when
awake is continually hungry. The one that doesn't like to
bathe or swim and can't dance. The one that goes to the
movies. The one that bites her nails. Call her Sue.

Two contradictory things brought out in me by K [*a friend,
and for some time a lover of SS's during this period*]: vitality,

by contrast with her lack of it; fear that her lack of it is contagious. Both sentiments are loathsome (each depends, feeds on the other).

Why don't I ever try to control things with I.? Consciously control, I mean. Not to conceal or evade, but just to make things better between us. I never do! Instead I let things drift, even provoke the sort of conversations that enflame us. "How is Alfred? What did you talk about?" etc. After four years, I should know where the land mines are. I do. But I'm lazy and self-destructive.

My aversion to manipulating, to seeing myself in conscious control—this is the source of X. X = the desire to place myself under the other's protection. In advance payment for this protection, I offer my amiable helplessness.

Work = being in the world

Loving, being loved = appreciating the world (but not being in it)

Unloved, unloving = finding the world tasteless, inanimate

Loving is the highest mode of valuing, preferring. But it's not a state of being

•

*[With no other comment, SS notes down the Cyrillic spellings of Lenin and Stalin.]*

•

*[Undated except "Sun. night," but clearly part of the Puerto Rico diary]*

This aching for I. the last two days—what is it made of? Sense of loss; frustration; resentment? That? And if that, only that? I feel her impenetrability—I can't grasp her. She eludes me, evades me—yet I can't stop wanting from her. Her judgments of me are like a thorn, an arrow, a barbed hook. I writhe. I want to get away + I want her to draw me in, both at the same time.

First off, I have to be calm. The business with Alfred poisons the air because I let it. If I could be generous (+ not so needy) I wouldn't care—either because I didn't care for Irene or because I did.

Either way I shouldn't mind.

What's burning me now? The reproach about no social life. With me every night she tells me she wants to work. That is, be downtown for her social club.

I hate I.['s] talk. I hate the way she's always making plans, + doing 1/10th of what she plans. I hate the way she stays in the tub for an hour + a half.—Not because I hate laziness or sloppiness, but because it doesn't go with her manness + tenseness. I hate the way she insists I listen to her.

4/10/63

Being with two, without denying (making a spectator out of) one! Why can't I do this? [*SS is presumably pondering her relationships with Irene Fornes and K.*]

Where does the hysteria—the compulsive assault of questions—come from? The desperate effort to make contact?

It's not that I want to prevent the two from getting together.
I'd be relieved, if they did. Yet I do everything to make it
impossible.

Always with one other—only one. This shows in my writing.
No scenes with three—

I'm so ashamed. I want to hide.


*[Undated, 1963]*

The look—more intimate (committing) than the sexual
embrace, because there is no room for detachment in it; the
gesture is too compact

.

The monstrously emasculated style of H[enry] J[ames]

.

Long voluptuous agony of indecision (every pain knows how
to find its pleasure!)

.

"Fun"—the American substitute for pleasure

8/8/63

fear of being left alone
no comfort, warmth, reassurance—
cold world—nothing to do

more anxiety when I lie down
stand up
take a bath

loss, loss, loss
life a holding operation

my insides are hollow

What will happen when David goes?

I wanted to get on a train tonight, so far away: FLIGHT

I'm afraid to take hold, afraid to let go

continual deceit > guilt > anxiety

. . .

How did everything go so wrong? How can I get myself out
of this mess?

. . . Do something
    Do something
    Do something

8/29/63

French vs. English

1. words from métiers [*e.g., various kinds of tools for work, etc.*] not absorbed into general language
2. fewer words (English a Siamese twin lang[uage])—everything doubled
3. vocabulary more abstract, fewer concrete words, esp[ecially] fewer verbs (fewer *active* verbs)
4. declarative style
5. metaphor less used
6. fewer words for immediate states of feeling

In French, one word follows another more obviously than in English—the choices are fewer.


*[Undated, but almost certainly September 1963]*

My [fiction] writing is always about dissociation—"I" and "it."

[The] problem of taking responsibility—This is treated mockingly in *The Benefactor*. Hippolyte serenely claims to be responsible for his acts, but patently is more haunted than he admits . . .

•

*The Benefactor* + the 2 stories are meditations on dissociative faits accomplis, their hazards + rewards.

[Jean] is enviable. He doesn't lose himself—he incorporates the world.

[Again] it's because it's always "I" vs. "it."

That there are no *people* in what I've written. Only ghosts.

*[Undated entry, late 1963]*

The intellectual ecstasy I have had access to since early childhood. But ecstasy is ecstasy.

Intellectual "wanting" like sexual wanting.